BLOOM

Olympiad ACE

A Comprehensive Practice Book

for School Olympiads & Talent Search Exams

MATHS

Class 8

by

Ajab Singh

Olympiad ACE

BLOOM

Bloom Cap Edu Ventures Pvt. Ltd.

Administrative & Production Office

'Ramchhaya' 4577/15, Agarwal Road, Darya Ganj, New Delhi -110002
Tele: 011- 47630600, 43518550

PRICE: ₹125.00

PO No. : TXT-59-T063323-02-25

Published by Arihant Publications (I) Ltd.

For further information about the books log on to
www.bloomcap.org

Follow us on

Preface

"Future belongs to those Who prepares for it today"

School Olympiads are National & International level competitions conducted by different Government, Non-Government & Educational Organisations with the purpose of making the children ready to face competitive exams. The challenging Questions asked in Olympiads motivate them to learn more & more and bring out the best result with improved academic performance. The Awards & Scholarship offered in Olympiads motivate children to aspire & strive for doing better and emerge out to be the best.

Maths Olympiads

Mathematics is an integral part of all competitive exams be it Aptitude or Commerce or Science. Maths Olympiads are meant to develop Mathematical aptitude in school students. They provide students with an opportunity to master their concepts and comprehend tricky questions effortlessly. Challenging Questions of Maths Olympiads encourage students to develop a logical approach to solve Mathematical Problems.

'Bloom Mathematics Olympiad Study Book Class 8' is a perfect resource to Study & Practice for Olympiad Exams and other National & State Level Talent Search Exams & Other Competitions.

Some Special Features of Bloom Maths Olympiad Study Books are;

- Chapterwise Exercises having different types of Objective Questions at par with the Olympiad Level.
- Detailed Explanation for each question.
- Olympiad Pattern Practice Sets at the end.

This book is prepared by Expert Panel with the utmost care, still if you have any suggestions regarding its improvement, then feel free to contact us at support@bloomcap.org. We will try to inculcate your suggestions in the further editions.

Contents

Chapter 01

Number System

1 Mark Questions

1. If $21y5$ is a multiple of 9, where y is a digit, then the value of y is

(a) 1 (b) 2
(c) 9 (d) 3

2. If A is a prime number greater than 20 and less than 50. What is the greatest possible value of A?

(a) 29 (b) 37
(c) 49 (d) 47

3. If 32 is expressed in terms of prime numbers. Which of the following expression is correct ?

(a) $26+6$
(b) $19+13$
(c) 8×4
(d) $11+21$

4. If the square of a number is having 9 at its units place and 4 its tenths place, then the least number having these properties are

(a) 49 (b) 79
(c) 7 (d) 69

5. If in a number, difference between the sum of digits at even places and that of odd places is 0, then the number is divisible, by ....

(a) 9 (b) 4
(c) 8 (d) 11

6. If a number $573xy$ is divisible by 90 [where, x, y is digit], then the value of $x+y$ is

(a) 8 (b) 3 (c) 5 (d) 7

7. The greatest value that must be given to z, so that the number $6542z8$ is divisible by 4 is

(a) 7 (b) 1 (c) 6 (d) 8

8. If N is divided by 5 leaves a remainder 0, then ones digit of N must be ?

(a) Either 1 or 4 (b) Either 5 or 1
(c) Either 0 or 5 (d) Either 0 or 4

9. Which of the following number is multiple of 8?

(a) 576248 (b) 679326
(c) 274913 (d) 213402

10. In 853 * 431, which number should be replaced the * to make the number divisible by 9?

(a) 3 (b) 4
(c) 5 (d) 9

11. The number 2735*46 is divisible by 11, where * is single digit number. What is/are the possible values of * ?

(a) 5 (b) 7
(c) 4 (d) 1

12. When N is divided by 4, the remainder is 3. What is the remainder when $2N$ is divided by 4?

(a) 2 (b) 3
(c) 4 (d) 8

13. If a six-digit number $93p25q$ is divisible by 88, then the value of p and q are respectively.

(a) 2 and 8
(b) 8 and 2
(c) 8 and 6
(d) 6 and 8

14. If $1^2 + 2^2 + 3^2 + \ldots\ldots + 512^2 = m$, then $2^2 + 4^2 + 6^2 + \ldots\ldots + 1024^2$ is equal to

(a) $3m$ (b) $4m$
(c) m^2 (d) m^3

15. P is a two-digit number. Q is the number obtained on reversing the digits of P. Which of the following is true?

(a) $P + Q$ is divisible by 8.
(b) $P - Q$ is divisible by 6.
(c) $P + Q$ is divisible by 12.
(d) $P - Q$ is divisible by 9.

2 Marks Questions

16. A 2-digit number has 3 at ones place and the sum of its digits is $\frac{1}{7}$ of the number itself. Then, the number is

(a) 43
(b) 53
(c) 63
(d) 73

17. If x is a digit such that the number $18x71$ is a multiple of 3, then the possible values of x are 4, 7 and

(a) 2 (b) 1
(c) 9 (d)5

18. Make a 5-digit number using each of the digits 4, 5, 6, 7, 8 (without repetition). Also, see that the number made shall be divisible by 33.

(a) 65478
(b) 45786
(c) 67584
(d) 75846

19. The product of 2-digit numbers is 1431. The product of their ten's digits is 10 and the product of their unit's digits is 21. Find the numbers.

(a) $9 \times \sqrt{3}$ (b) 53×27
(c) Both (a) and (b) (d) None of these

20. State 'T' for true or 'F' for false.

I. The sum of two consecutive odd number is always divisible by 4.
II. If a number is divisible by 4, it must be divisible by 2.
III. If a number is not divisible by 4 and 5, it is divisible by 20.
IV. Last 3-digit of a number must be divisible by 4 to check 4's divisibility.

Codes

	I	II	III	IV
(a)	T	T	F	F
(b)	F	T	F	F
(c)	T	T	T	F
(d)	T	F	F	T

Chapter 02

Rational Number

1 Mark Questions

1. A rational number, which is less than every positive real number and greater than every negative rational number, is

(a) -1 (b) 1

(c) Can't say (d) 0

2. Which of the following rational numbers has no reciprocal?

(a) $\frac{3}{5}$ (b) $\frac{7}{9}$ (c) 0 (d) $\frac{5}{9}$

3. Which one of the following is a natural number?

(a) $\frac{15}{60}$ (b) $\frac{17}{51}$

(c) $\frac{81}{27}$ (d) $\frac{25}{35}$

4. In the given figure,

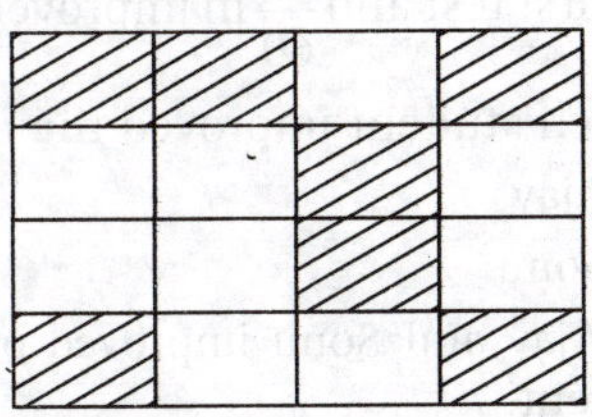

The shaded area can be represented as the fraction of whole figure in p/q form. The fraction will be

(a) $\frac{1}{2}$ (b) $\frac{8}{16}$

(c) $\frac{7}{16}$ (d) $\frac{8}{15}$

5. $\left(\frac{2}{5}+\frac{15}{25}-5\right)+\left(\frac{7}{15}\right)$ is equal to

(a) $\frac{53}{15}$ (b) $\frac{1}{15}$

(c) $-\frac{53}{15}$ (d) $-\frac{1}{15}$

6. The sum of two rational numbers is (-3). If one of them is $\left(-\frac{6}{7}\right)$. Then, other number is

(a) $\frac{15}{7}$ (b) $-\frac{15}{7}$

(c) $\frac{27}{7}$ (d) $-\frac{27}{7}$

7. If $a=\frac{1}{5}$, then the value of $\left\{-\left(-\frac{a-1}{a}\right)\right\}$ is

(a) $\frac{4}{5}$ (b) $-\frac{4}{5}$

(c) $-\frac{1}{\frac{1}{4}}$ (d) $-\frac{1}{4}$

8. If the fraction $4 + \cfrac{1}{m + \cfrac{1}{n}}$ is equivalent to the fraction $\frac{56}{12}$. Then, the value of $m + n$, where m and n are integers, is

(a) 2 (b) 3 (c) 5 (d) 8

9. Dividing the sum of $\frac{77}{14}$ and $\frac{195}{26}$ by their difference, we get the positive number as

(a) $\frac{2}{13}$ (b) $\frac{19}{3}$

(c) $\frac{13}{2}$ (d) None of these

10. The value of $\frac{2}{5} \times \frac{-3}{7} - \frac{1}{14} - \frac{3}{7} \times \frac{3}{5}$ is equal to

(a) $\frac{1}{3}$ (b) $\frac{3}{21}$

(c) $-\frac{1}{2}$ (d) None of these

11. The property of multiplication of rational numbers illustrated by the following statement is

$$-\frac{5}{2} \times \frac{3}{4} + \frac{-5}{2} \times \frac{-6}{7} = \frac{-5}{2} \times \left(\frac{3}{4} - \frac{6}{7}\right)$$

(a) Associative (b) Distributive

(c) Commutative (d) None of these

12. **Assertion** (A) $a - (b - c) = (a - b) - c$

Reason (R) Rational numbers are not associative under subtraction.

Which of the following is true?

(a) Both (A) and (R) are true and (R) is correct explanation of (A)

(b) Both (A) and (R) are false and (R) is not correct explanation of (A)

(c) (A) is true and (R) is false

(d) (A) is false and (R) is true

13. If difference of $\frac{3}{5}$ and $\frac{2}{7}$ of a number is 44. Then, the sum of digits of that number is

(a) 50 (b) 5

(c) 14 (d) 4

14. If 16 shirts of equal size can be made out of 24 m cloth. The length of cloth needed for making 12 such shirts is

(a) 15 m (b) 18 m

(c) 24 m (d) 12 m

15. 2/5th of the total number of students of a school come by car, while 1/4th of rest of the students come to school by bus and the remaining 180 students come by walking. The total number of students is

(a) 500 (b) 450

(c) 400 (d) 300

16. Raju earns ₹ 12000 per month, he spends $\frac{1}{4}$ of his income on food, $\frac{3}{10}$ of remaining money on house rent. The money saved by Raju is

(a) ₹ 4500 (b) ₹ 6300

(c) ₹ 5000 (d) ₹ 1200

17. Three students gave an improvement test. Ajay scored $\frac{30}{60}$ in his first test and $\frac{35}{60}$ in improvement test. Sonu scored $\frac{42}{70}$ in his first test and $\frac{50}{60}$ in improvement test.

Which student improved the most?

(a) Ajay

(b) Sonu

(c) Ajay and Sonu improved by same per cent.

(d) None of the above

18. State 'T' for true or 'F' for false.

I. If $\frac{p}{q}$ is a rational number, then $p \neq 0$.

II. If $\frac{b}{a}$ is multiplicative inverse of $\frac{a}{b}$, then $a \neq 0$.

III. For any rational number $x, x+(-1)=-x$.

IV. $\frac{x+y}{2}$ is a rational number which lies between x and y.

V. If $\frac{p}{q}=\frac{3}{5}$ and $\frac{x}{y}=\frac{2}{3}$, then $\frac{py+qx}{3qy}=\frac{19}{45}$

Codes

	I	II	III	IV	V
(a)	F	T	F	T	T
(b)	T	F	T	F	F
(c)	F	F	F	F	F
(d)	T	T	T	T	T

2 Marks Questions

19. On subtracting the sum of $\frac{-4}{7}$ and $\frac{5}{14}$ from the sum of $\frac{9}{14}$ and $\frac{23}{14}$, we get

(a) $\frac{2}{5}$ (b) $\frac{5}{7}$

(c) $\frac{5}{2}$ (d) $\frac{3}{5}$

20. The sum of $\frac{-4}{7}+\frac{7}{6}+\frac{2}{7}+3+\frac{-11}{6}$ is equal to

(a) $\frac{21}{43}$ (b) $\frac{43}{21}$ (c) $\frac{23}{43}$ (d) $\frac{43}{23}$

21. Fill in the blanks with the help of options, given in the box.

(i) x^4,	(ii) $-\frac{7}{5}$,
(iii) $\frac{8}{3}$,	(iv) $-\frac{3}{2}$,
(v) 1,	(vi) 10,
(vii) -1,	(viii) $\frac{3}{2}$,
(ix) $\frac{6}{3}$,	(x) $-\frac{5}{7}$,
(xi) $\frac{9}{13}$,	(xii) 0

I. $-(-2)\div 2^{-1}\times 2+2=$ ____ .

II. $\left(\frac{3}{2}-\frac{2}{3}\right)-(-\square)=-\frac{1}{6}$.

III. If $m * n=\frac{m}{n}-\frac{n}{m}$, then $9 * 18=$ ____ .

IV. $\left(\frac{1}{4}+\frac{3}{2}\right)\div\left(\frac{1}{4}-\frac{3}{2}\right)$ is ____ .

Codes

	I	II	III	IV
(a)	(i)	(ii)	(iii)	(v)
(b)	(vi)	(vii)	(iv)	(ii)
(c)	(vi)	(vii)	(viii)	(x)
(d)	(xi)	(xii)	(i)	(iii)

22. If the number $3254p06q$ is exactly divisible by 3 and 5, then the maximum value of $p+q$ is

(a) 12 (b) 13 (c) 14 (d) 15

23. The following table:

	Items		Cost
I.	Hot dog	(i)	5 for ₹ 60
II.	Pastry	(ii)	4 for ₹ 20
III.	Roll	(iii)	3 for ₹ 60

Ronak bought 3 hot dogs, 2 pastries and 4 rolls. If he has total ₹ 200 in his pocket, then money left to the total money is represented in the form of $\left(\frac{p}{q}\right)$ i.e. rational number is

(a) $\frac{37}{50}$ (b) $\frac{74}{200}$

(c) $\frac{126}{200}$ (d) None of these

24. One recipe requires 2/5 cup of sugar. Another recipe for the same dish requires 5 tablespoons of sugar. If 1 tablespoon is equivalent to 1/15 cup, then the more amount of sugar needed by the first recipe is

(a) 1 tablespoon

(b) 15 tablespoons

(c) 1/5 cup

(d) 5 tablespoons

25. Mohan and Sohan each receives an annual allowance. The table shows the fraction of their allowance they used as follows:

		Fraction of allowance	
		Mohan	**Sohan**
I.	Saving account	$\frac{1}{2}$	$\frac{1}{3}$
II.	Spend at mall	...	$\frac{3}{5}$
III.	Left over	₹ 84	₹ 84

If total allowance is ₹1260 to each of them, then what will come in place of ...?

(a) $\frac{7}{15}$ (b) $\frac{13}{30}$

(c) $\frac{14}{30}$ (d) $\frac{9}{15}$

Chapter
03

Square and Square Roots

1 Mark Questions

1. If m is the square of a natural number n, then n is
(a) the square of m
(b) greater than m
(c) equal to m
(d) equal to $\sqrt{m}$

2. Which of the following is not a perfect square?
(a) 36 (b) 196
(c) 181 (d) 169

3. Which of the following cannot be the last digit (unit's place) in a perfect square number?
(a) 1 (b) 0
(c) 5 (d) 7

4. Which of the following letter best represents the location of $x - y$, where $x = \sqrt{169}$ and $y = \sqrt{64}$?

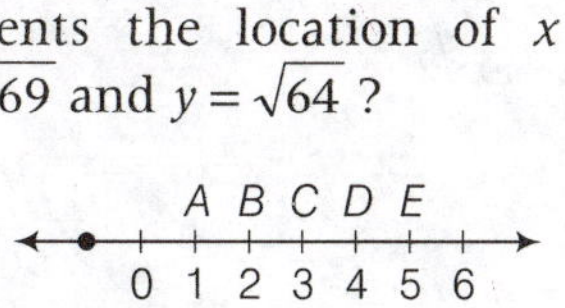

(a) B (b) A
(c) D (d) E

5. The sum of successive odd numbers from 1 to 20 is
(a) 81 (b) 100
(c) 64 (d) 49

6. It is given that $\sqrt{4761} = 69$, then the value of $\sqrt{4761} + \sqrt{47.61} + \sqrt{0.4761}$ is
(a) 77 (b) 75.59
(c) 76.59 (d) 70.59

7. The value of expression $\sqrt{248 + \sqrt{52 + \sqrt{144}}}$ is
(a) 14 (b) 12
(c) 16 (d) 13

8. If $\sqrt{2 + \sqrt{x}} = 3$, then the value of x is
(a) 1 (b) $\sqrt{7}$
(c) $\sqrt{49}$ (d) 49

9. If $\sqrt{188 + \sqrt{53 + \sqrt{y}}} = 14$, then the value of y is
(a) 121 (b) 11
(c) 1331 (d) 161

10. If $\sqrt{1 + \frac{27}{169}} = \left(1 + \frac{x}{13}\right)$, then the value of x is
(a) 1 (b) 3
(c) 5 (d) 7

11. The square root of $\frac{1.69}{0.0036} \times \frac{1.44}{6.76}$ is
(a) 10 (b) 10.2
(c) 10.6 (d) 9.8

12. The two other numbers forming a Pythagorean triplet, whose third number is 5, then find the other two numbers.
(a) (3, 4) (b) (–3, 5)
(c) (6, 4) (d) (3, 7)

13. The greatest five-digit number, which is a perfect square, is
(a) 99746 (b) 99856
(c) 90456 (d) 99999

14. A person borrowed some money from a friend and promised him to pay daily for 1 month. He will pay like ₹ 1 for first day, ₹ 3 for second day, ₹ 5 for third day and so on for 30 days. If he paid an interest of ₹ 150 included in the above amount, then the money borrowed by him is
(a) ₹ 600 (b) ₹ 750
(c) ₹ 900 (d) ₹ 1200

15. The smallest square number which is exactly divisible by each of the numbers 6, 9 and 15, is
(a) 100 (b) 400
(c) 900 (d) 1024

16. The smallest number by which 396 must be multiplied so that the product becomes a perfect square.
(a) 9 (b) 10
(c) 11 (d) 13

17. What least number should be added to the number 6800, so that the resultant number is a perfect square?
(a) 24 (b) 76
(c) 89 (d) 256

18. What least number must be subtracted from 5190 to make it a perfect square.
(a) 10 (b) 6
(c) 28 (d) 21

19. A group of students in a class collects ₹ 9216. The amount contributed by each student is equivalent to the number of students in the class. Then, total number of students is
(a) 43
(b) 53
(c) 96
(d) 66

2 Marks Questions

20. If three numbers are in the ratio 1 : 2 : 3 and the sum of their squares is 224. Then, the difference between the squares of greatest and least numbers is
(a) 80
(b) 160
(c) 128
(d) 240

21. If $a = \sqrt{2} + 1$ and $b = \sqrt{2} - 1$, then the value of expression $\dfrac{a^2 - ab + b^2}{a^2 + ab + b^2}$ is
(a) $32 - 4\sqrt{2}$
(b) $32 + 4\sqrt{2}$
(c) 0
(d) 5/7

22. State 'T' for true or 'F' for false.

I. The sum of two perfect squares is a perfect square.

II. The sum of first n even numbers is n^2.

III. When a square number ends with 6, then the number whose square it is, will have either 4 or 7 in unit's place.

IV. The general form of Pythagorean triplet is $m^2 - 1, m^2 + 1, 2m + 1$.

V. The square of a prime number is not a prime number.

Codes

	I	II	III	IV	V
(a)	F	F	F	F	T
(b)	T	F	T	F	T
(c)	T	T	T	T	T
(d)	F	T	F	T	F

23. Fill in the blanks with the help of options, given in the box.

(i) 169, (ii) 144, (iii) 200, (iv) 400
(v) 25, (vi) 8, 15, (vii) 16, (viii) 9,
(ix) 20, (x) 1, (xi) 4

I. $1+3+5+7+9+11+13+15+17+19+21+23$ is ___ (find without adding)

II. The value of $101^2 - 99^2$ is ___

III. The value of $\sqrt{610+\sqrt{212+\sqrt{169}}}$ is

IV. The sides of a right angled triangle, whose hypotenuse is 17 cm, are ___ and ___ .

Codes

	I	II	III	IV
(a)	(ii)	(iv)	(v)	(vi)
(b)	(i)	(ii)	(iii)	(iv)
(c)	(vii)	(viii)	(ix)	(x)
(d)	(ii)	(iii)	(iv)	(v)

24. Match the following.

	Column I		Column II
I.	Smallest perfect square	(i)	17
II.	Sum of first 8 odd numbers	(ii)	1
III.	Area of square is 144 cm^2, its perimeter is	(iii)	64
IV.	The least number added to sum of squares of first 5 prime numbers to form a perfect square	(iv)	48

Codes

	I	II	III	IV
(a)	(i)	(ii)	(iii)	(iv)
(b)	(iii)	(ii)	(iv)	(i)
(c)	(iii)	(iv)	(ii)	(i)
(d)	(ii)	(iii)	(iv)	(i)

Chapter 04

Cube and Cube Roots

1 Mark Questions

1. Which of the following is a cube of negative number?

(a) 1331 (b) – 729
(c) 3375 (d) – 1724

2. Which of the following numbers is a perfect cube?

(a) 1331 (b) 1441
(c) 3475 (d) 2285

3. The cube root of 3.375 is

(a) 0.15 (b) 1.5
(c) 15 (d) 2.5

4. $\frac{14}{15}$ is the cube root of which of the following number?

(a) $\frac{-2744}{3375}$ (b) $\frac{32764}{4485}$
(c) $\frac{2744}{3375}$ (d) $\frac{-3375}{2744}$

5. The cube root of $(-125) \times (-3375)$ is

(a) 65 (b) – 75
(c) – 85 (d) 75

6. The value of the expression $\sqrt[3]{27} + \sqrt[3]{0.008} + \sqrt[3]{0.064}$ is

(a) 9.7 (b) 3.6
(c) 6.3 (d) 4.8

7. If 32* K (where * means multiplication) gives a perfect cube, then the value of K is

(a) 3 (b) 2
(c) 5 (d) 8

8. The value of the expression $\sqrt[3]{288} \times \sqrt[3]{432} \times \sqrt[3]{648}$ is

(a) 432 (b) 565
(c) 469 (d) 328

9. By what smallest number should 243 be divided, so that the quotient be a perfect cube?

(a) 81
(b) 3
(c) 9
(d) None of the above

10. If cube of a number x is four times of x, then value of x, where $x > 0$, is

(a) 8 (b) 2
(c) 4 (d) 3

11. If surface area of a cube is 150 cm^2, then the volume of the cube will be

(a) 25 cm^3
(b) 75 cm^3
(c) 125 cm^3
(d) 27 cm^3

12. In the given five-digit number $1A6B3$, B is the greatest single digit perfect cube and twice of it exceeds A by 7.

Then, the sum of the above number and its cube root is

(a) 18700 (b) 11862
(c) 19710 (d) 25320

13. To collect rainwater, Sonia made a cubical tank which can hold 10648 m^3 water. She uses this water for watering the plants of her garden. What is the height of the tank?

(a) 21 m (b) 22 m
(c) 23 m (d) 27 m

14. State 'T' for true or 'F' for false.

I. For any positive number n, $n^2 < n^3$.
II. Hardy-Ramanujan numbers can't be expressed as a sum of two cubes in two different ways.
III. As the square of negative number is positive, similarly the cube of negative number is also positive.
IV. For two natural numbers a and b, $a^3 \times b^3 = (a \times b)^3$.

Codes

	I	II	III	IV		I	II	III	IV
(a)	T	F	F	T	(b)	T	T	F	T
(c)	F	F	T	F	(d)	F	T	T	T

2 Marks Questions

15. Find the total surface area of a cube whose volume is 24389 cm^3.

(a) 4956 cm^2
(b) 5046 cm^2
(c) 5126 cm^2
(d) 4756 cm^2

16. Three numbers are in the ratio 2 : 3 : 4 to one another. The sum of their cubes is 33957. Then, the difference in the cubes of greatest and smallest numbers is

(a) 20000
(b) 21200
(c) 19208
(d) 22208

17. **Assertion** (A) 1729 is a Hardy-Ramanujan number.

Reason (R) Cube of 12 is 1728.

Which of the following is true?

(a) Both (A) and (R) are true and (R) is correct explanation of (A)
(b) Both (A) and (R) are true but (R) is not the correct explanation of (A)
(c) (A) is true and (R) is false
(d) (A) is false and (R) is true

18. Match the following.

	Column I		Column II
I.	$\sqrt[6]{\left(\frac{91125}{216}\right)^2}$	(i)	9
II.	Smallest cubic number is	(ii)	$\frac{8}{5}$
III.	If $\sqrt[3]{4\frac{12}{125}} = x$, then x is	(iii)	1
IV.	If $(27)^{1/3} = 3$, then $\sqrt[3]{729}$ is	(iv)	45/6

Codes

	I	II	III	IV
(a)	(i)	(ii)	(iii)	(iv)
(b)	(iv)	(iii)	(ii)	(i)
(c)	(iv)	(ii)	(iii)	(i)
(d)	(ii)	(iv)	(i)	(iii)

19. If $\sqrt[3]{3\left(\sqrt[3]{x} - \frac{1}{\sqrt[3]{x}}\right)} = 2$, then the value of $\left(x - \frac{1}{x}\right)$ is

(a) $\frac{728}{9}$ (b) $\frac{72}{27}$ (c) $\frac{728}{27}$ (d) $\frac{3}{15}$

Chapter

05

Exponents and Powers

1 Mark Questions

1. For a non-zero integer x, $(x^4)^{-3}$ is equal to

(a) x^{12} (b) x^{-12} (c) x^{64} (d) x^{-64}

2. The value of $-(-2)^3-(-3)^2+(-3)^4$ is equal to

(a) 80 (b) 64

(c) -82 (d) None of these

3. If $2^x+2^x+2^x=192$, then the value of x is

(a) 5 (b) 6

(c) 9 (d) 3

4. The value of $[1^{-2}+2^{-2}+3^{-2}]\times 6^2$ is equal to

(a) 50 (b) 49

(c) 1/49 (d) 37

5. The value of given expression

$$(a^m \cdot a^n) \div (a^m / a^n)$$

is equal to, if $a=2$ and $m, n \in$ integers.

(a) 2^{2m+2n} (b) 2^{2n}

(c) 2^{2m} (d) None of these

6. Simplify $(9cp^{-3})^{-2}$.

(a) $\dfrac{p^6}{81c^2}$ (b) $\dfrac{c^2}{81p^2}$

(c) $\dfrac{p^2}{729c^3}$ (d) $\dfrac{c^6}{81p^2}$

7. What is the standard form of 0.0000000007973?

(a) 7.973×10^{12} (b) 79.73×10^{-11}

(c) 7973×10^{13} (d) 7.973×10^{-12}

8. If $\dfrac{(-2)^x\times(-2)^7}{3\times4^6}=\dfrac{1}{12}$, then the value of x is

(a) 3 (b) -3

(c) 2 (d) -4

9. If $\dfrac{5^m\times5^3\times5^{-2}}{5^{-3}\times5^{-2}}=5^{12}$, then the value of m is

(a) 4 (b) 5

(c) 6 (d) 3

10. If $10^m\times10^n\times10^p=10^6$, then the average of m, n and p is

(a) 0 (b) 1

(c) 3 (d) 2

11. What will come in the places of x and y respectively?

$(36)^{1/2}$ — $\times(3)^2$ — $\div(27)^{1/3}$ — $=3^x\times2^y$

(a) 1, 2

(b) 2, 1

(c) 3, 0

(d) None of the above

12. The value of $\frac{2^{2004}-2^{2003}}{2^{2004}+2^{2003}}$ is equal to

(a) 0 (b) 2^{-2006}
(c) $\frac{1}{3}$ (d) $\frac{1}{2}$

13. If $4^x+4^x+4^x+4^x=\frac{1}{256}$, then the value of $-\frac{3}{x}$ is

(a) -5 (b) -8
(c) -0.75 (d) -4.25

14. If $\frac{8^{x+1}}{2^{x-x}}=64$, then the value of 3^{2x+1} is equal to

(a) 1 (b) 3
(c) 9 (d) 27

15. If $3^x\times\frac{10}{3}-3^{x-1}=81$, then the value of x is

(a) 2 (b) 1
(c) 3 (d) 0

16. The cells of a bacterium double itself every hour. How many cells will there be after 10 h, if initially it is one cell?

(a) 512 (b) 256
(c) 1024 (d) 20

17. Find the sum of the powers of the prime factors in 512×448.

(a) 12 (b) 15
(c) 16 (d) 14

18. The value of $\sqrt{2\frac{1}{4}\times\left(1\frac{1}{3}\right)^2+1\div\sqrt[3]{3\frac{3}{8}}}$ is

(a) $3\frac{1}{3}$ (b) $4\frac{1}{6}$
(c) $1\frac{1}{3}$ (d) $5\frac{1}{2}$

19. Simplified form of the expression $\frac{2\cdot3^{n+1}+7\cdot3^{n-1}}{3^{n+2}-2\left(\frac{1}{3}\right)^{1-n}}$ is

(a) 1 (b) 3
(c) -1 (d) 0

20. Assertion (A) $2^5\div2^2=8$

Reason (R) $a^m\div a^n=a^{m-n}$, according to the exponent rule.

Which of the following is true?

(a) Both (A) and (R) are true and (R) is the correct explanation of (A)
(b) Both (A) and (R) are false and (R) is not the correct explanation of (A)
(c) (A) is true and (R) is false
(d) (A) is false and (R) is true

21. State 'T' for true or 'F' for false.

I. For any non-zero integer a, $a^{-m}=\frac{1}{a^m}$.

II. $(-1)^0=-1$

III. The standard form for 0.0000048 is 4.8×10^{-6}.

IV. The $\frac{p}{q}$ form of the solution of $(4^{-1}+8^{-1})\div\left(\frac{2}{3}\right)^{-1}$ is $\frac{1}{8}$.

V. The reciprocal of $\left(\frac{2}{3}\right)^4$ is $\left(\frac{3}{2}\right)^4$.

Codes

	I	II	III	IV	V
(a)	T	T	T	T	F
(b)	F	F	T	F	F
(c)	T	F	T	F	T
(d)	F	F	T	T	T

2 Marks Questions

22. The value of m for which $\frac{(16)^{2m+1} \cdot (64)^5}{4} = (256)^{3m+2}$, is

(a) 1 (b) 0
(c) 4 (d) 5

23. Find the value of $A+B$ by the given expression
$(6^{30} + 6^{-30})(6^{30} - 6^{-30}) = 3^A \cdot 8^B - 3^{-A} \cdot 8^{-B}$ is

(a) 30 (b) 40
(c) 60 (d) 80

24. The value of the expression $\left(\frac{81}{16}\right)^{-3/4} \times \left[\left(\frac{25}{9}\right)^{-3/2} \div \left(\frac{5}{2}\right)^{-3}\right]$ is

(a) $\frac{6}{25}$ (b) $\frac{12}{125}$
(c) 1 (d) $-\left(\frac{5}{2}\right)^{-3}$

25. Fill in the blanks with the help of options given in the box.

(i) $-\left(\frac{1}{2}\right)^5$, (ii) $\frac{1}{81}$, (iii) 3, (iv) different, (v) $\left(\frac{5}{8}\right)$, (vi) same, (vii) 1, (viii) 0

I. $(-2)^{-5}$ is same as ___ .
II. The value of 4^{-2} and $(-2)^4$ are ___ .
III. $\left(\frac{8}{5}\right)^{-3} \div \left(\frac{5}{8}\right)^2 =$ ___ .
IV. If $\left(\frac{5}{2}\right)^{-4} \times \left(\frac{5}{2}\right)^{13} = \left(\frac{5}{2}\right)^{3x}$, then $x =$ ___ .
V. $\left[\left\{\left(-\frac{1}{3}\right)^2\right\}^{-2}\right]^{-1} =$ ___ .

Codes

	I	II	III	IV	V
(a)	(i)	(iv)	(v)	(iii)	(ii)
(b)	(ii)	(iii)	(iv)	(v)	(vi)
(c)	(vii)	(viii)	(i)	(ii)	(iii)
(d)	(iv)	(v)	(vi)	(vii)	(iii)

26. Match the following:

	Column I		Column II
I.	$\left(-\frac{3}{2}\right)^3 \times x = \left(\frac{4}{27}\right)^{-2} \Rightarrow x =$	(i)	-32
II.	$\frac{6^n}{6^{-2}} = 6^3 \Rightarrow n =$	(ii)	n
III.	$4^{n-1} = \frac{1}{4} \cdot 4^y \Rightarrow y =$	(iii)	1
IV.	$-(3)^3 - (-3)^2 + (-2)^2 =$	(iv)	$\frac{(-3)^3}{2}$

Codes

	I	II	III	IV
(a)	(i)	(ii)	(iii)	(iv)
(b)	(iv)	(iii)	(ii)	(i)
(c)	(iii)	(iv)	(i)	(ii)
(d)	(iv)	(iii)	(i)	(ii)

Chapter

06

Percentage

1 Mark Questions

1. If 16% of a number is 72, then find the number.
(a) 480 (b) 450
(c) 350 (d) 360

2. A period of 4 h 30 min is what percent of a day?
(a) $18\frac{3}{4}\%$ (b) 20%
(c) $16\frac{2}{3}\%$ (d) 19%

3. A man saves 18% of his monthly income. If he saves ₹ 3780 per month, then what is his monthly income?
(a) ₹ 24000 (b) ₹ 28000
(c) ₹ 21000 (d) ₹ 36000

4. A football team wins 7 games, which is 35% of the total games played. How many games were played in all?
(a) 20 (b) 24
(c) 32 (d) 36

5. Sonal attended her school on 204 days in a full year. If her attendance is 85%, then find the number of days on which the school was opened.
(a) 250 (b) 240 (c) 270 (d) 300

6. A cricket team won 60% of the total matches it played during the year. If it lost 24 matches in all and no matches were drawn, then find the number of matches played during the year.
(a) 45 (b) 54 (c) 60 (d) 72

7. The sum of two numbers is 4000. 10% of one number is $6\frac{2}{3}\%$ of the other. The difference of the numbers is
(a) 600 (b) 800 (c) 1025 (d) 1175

8. A candidate who gets 20% marks in an examination fail by 30 marks but another candidate who gets 32%, get 42 marks more than the pass marks. The percentage of pass marks is
(a) 52% (b) 50%
(c) 33% (d) 25%

9. The value of a machine depreciates every year by 20%. If the present value of the machine be ₹ 240000, then what was its value last year?
(a) ₹ 200000 (b) ₹ 250000
(c) ₹ 300000 (d) ₹ 325000

10. A beaker containing 475 L of kerosene oil last 8% by leakage an evaporation. Find the number of litres of kerosene oil left in the beaker?
(a) 491 L (b) 431 L
(c) 437 L (d) 425 L

11. Which is largest in $6\frac{2}{3}\%$, $\frac{3}{20}$ and 0.14?

(a) $6\frac{2}{3}$

(b) $\frac{3}{20}$

(c) 0.14

(d) None of the above

12. Balanced diet should contain 12% of proteins, 25% of fats and 63% of carbohydrates. If a child needs 2600 calories in his food daily, then find in calories the amount of carbohydrates in his daily food intake.

(a) 1548 calories
(b) 1638 calories
(c) 1432 calories
(d) 1256 calories

13. An alloy contains 40% copper, 32% nickel and rest zinc. Find the mass of zinc in 1 kg of the alloy.

(a) 320 g (b) 240 g
(c) 300 g (d) 280 g

14. There are 80 coins of ₹ 5 in the purse. These coins constitute 20% of its total coins. How many coins are there in the purse?

(a) 400 (b) 320
(c) 480 (d) 240

15. *A*'s income is 20% less than that of *B*. By what percent is *B*'s income more than *A*'s?

(a) 20% (b) $16\frac{2}{3}\%$
(c) $14\frac{2}{7}\%$ (d) 25%

2 Marks Questions

16. Find the percentage of pure gold in 22-carat gold, if 24-carat gold is 100% pure.

(a) $33\frac{1}{3}\%$ (b) $66\frac{2}{3}\%$
(c) $37\frac{1}{2}\%$ (d) $91\frac{2}{3}\%$

17. Gunpowder contains 75% nitre and 10% sulphur. Find the amount of gunpowder which carries 9 kg nitre. What amount of gunpowder would contain 2.5 kg sulphur?

(a) 24 kg and 27 kg
(b) 10 kg and 18 kg
(c) 15 kg and 27 kg
(d) 12 kg and 25 kg

18. Divide ₹ 7000 among *A*, *B* and *C* such that *A* gets 50% of what *B* gets and *B* gets 50% of what *C* gets. Find the amount getting by the *B*.

(a) ₹ 2000 (b) ₹ 2500
(c) ₹ 1000 (d) ₹ 3500

19. Fill in the blanks.

I. $7\frac{1}{2}\%$ of ₹ 1200 = ...

II. 240 ml is .... % of 3 L.

III. If $x\%$ of 35 is 42, then x = ...

IV. 120 = (........%) of 80

(i) ₹ 90, (ii) $12\frac{1}{2}\%$, (iii) ₹ 150,
(iv) 240%, (v) ₹ 2000, (vi) $-\frac{3}{5}$,
(vii) 150%, (viii) 8%,
(ix) ₹ 120, (x) 120%

Codes

	I	II	III	IV
(a)	(v)	(i)	(ix)	(ii)
(b)	(i)	(viii)	(vii)	(x)
(c)	(iii)	(i)	(x)	(vii)
(d)	(i)	(viii)	(x)	(vii)

Chapter 07

Ratio and Proportion

1 Mark Questions

1. In case of direct variation, between x and y, which of the following is true?

(a) $xy = K$ (b) $\frac{x}{y} = K$

(c) $\frac{K}{y} = x$ (d) $\frac{x}{K} = y$

2. If x and y are directly proportional and when $x = 10$, $y = 25$, then which of the following is a possible pair of corresponding values of x and y?

(a) 1 and 3 (b) 2 and 5

(c) 15 and 60 (d) 4 and 8

3. What is the ratio of 50 g and 2 kg?

(a) 1 : 40 (b) 3 : 40

(c) 5 : 80 (d) 2 : 82

4. If $A:B = 3:4$ and $B:C = 6:5$, then find the value of $A:B:C$.

(a) 9 : 6 : 10 (b) 9 : 12 : 10

(c) 6 : 12 : 10 (d) 9 : 8 : 10

5. The angles of a triangle are in ratio $4:5:9$. Then, the angles are

(a) 20°, 110°, 50°

(b) 40°, 60°, 80°

(c) 40°, 50°, 90°

(d) 45°, 45°, 90°

6. A car needs 54 L of diesel for covering a distance of 297 km. How much more diesel required to cover a distance of 550 km?

(a) 100 L (b) 50 L

(c) 46 L (d) 25 L

7. Observe the following and choose the correct option.

x	6	12	18	24	15	9
y	4	8	12	16	10	6

(a) $x \propto y$ (b) $x \propto \frac{1}{y}$

(c) $xy = K$ (d) $x \neq y$

8. In a camp, there are 100 persons and there is food available for 24 days for all of them. Due to some reasons, 20 persons come into the camp. How many days they will enjoy the food?

(a) 10 (b) 15

(c) 20 (d) 30

9. A school has 8 periods in a day each of 30 min duration. What will be duration of each period, if school has decided to 10 periods a day and keep the school hours same?

(a) 30 min (b) 24 min

(c) 25 min (d) 20 min

10. A factory employing 300 men assembles a given number of TV sets weekly, the number of working hours being 60 per week. How many men would be required for the same production, if the working hours are 40 per week?

(a) 400 (b) 450
(c) 500 (d) 300

11. Typing at 30 words per minute, Aman will be able to finish his essay in 2 h. His friend Kali says that she should be able to finish it in one and a half hours. At what speed must she able to type?

(a) 40 (b) 38
(c) 42 (d) 45

12. A shopkeeper has first enough money to buy 50 fans worth ₹ 500 each. If each fan were to cost ₹ 20 more, then number of fans, he will able to buy with that amount of money (approx), is

(a) 50 (b) 45
(c) 48 (d) 40

13. If 8 persons complete a piece of work in 6 days. Then, how many days it will take to complete the same work by 6 persons?

(a) 12 (b) 8
(c) 18 (d) 3

14. 60 cows graze a field in 15 days. How many cows will graze the field in 10 days?

(a) 70 (b) 90
(c) 120 (d) 30

15. Dinesh goes to school at an average speed of 12 km/h and reach the school in 20 min. If he wants to reach his school in 15 min, then what should be his average speed?

(a) 8 km/h (b) 16 km/h
(c) 12 km/h (d) 20 km/h

16. A train covers a distance of 30 km in 30 min. How much time it will take to cover a distance of 15 km?

(a) 1 h (b) $\frac{1}{4}$ h
(c) $\frac{1}{3}$ h (d) $\frac{1}{2}$ h

17. A man can complete $\frac{5}{8}$ of a work in 10 days. At this rate, how many extra days will it take to complete $\frac{3}{4}$ of that work?

(a) 12 (b) 16 (c) 2 (d) 6

18. State 'T' for true or 'F' for false.

I. When two quantities x and y are in direct proportion, then xy is constant.

II. Length of a side of a square and its area are directly proportional to each other.

III. If x and y are inversely proportional, then $(x+1)$ and $(y+1)$ are also in inversely proportional.

IV. For a fixed time period and rate of interest, the simple interest is directly proportional to the principal.

Codes

	I	II	III	IV
(a)	F	T	T	T
(b)	T	F	T	F
(c)	T	T	T	T
(d)	F	F	F	F

2 Marks Questions

19. A car needs 33 L of petrol to cover a distance of 363 km. Petrol costs ₹ 78 per litre. How much would one spend on a journey of 407 km by that car ?

(a) ₹ 2996 (b) ₹ 2773

(c) ₹ 3286 (d) ₹ 2886

20. The ratio of ages of a son and his mother 5 yr ago was 2 : 5. After 5 yr, the ratio will become 4 : 7. The present age of son is

(a) 10 yr (b) 15 yr

(c) 20 yr (d) 8 yr

21. In the festive season, company A launches an offer on his products. The offer is, you can buy either two watches or three fans in ₹ 1500. Ram wants to buy 6 fans and 6 watches. How much money he needs to buy this?

(a) ₹ 10000

(b) ₹ 7500

(c) ₹ 9000

(d) ₹ 10500

22. Fill in the blanks with the help of options, given in the box.

(i) directly proportional,	(ii) decreases,
(iii) 8:15,	(iv) no variation,
(v) direct,	(vi) increase,
(vii) 15:8,	(viii) indirect,
(ix) 1:6,	(x) 12:1

I. The expenditure on petrol is ___ to the consumption.

II. For $xy = 5$, if x increases, then y ___ .

III. If $A:B = 2:3$, $B:C = 4:5$, then $A:C =$ ___ .

IV. If $\frac{1}{x} = \frac{x}{9}$ and $\frac{y}{2} = \frac{2}{16}$, then $x:y =$ ___ .

Codes

	I	II	III	IV
(a)	(v)	(ii)	(iii)	(iv)
(b)	(i)	(ii)	(iii)	(x)
(c)	(viii)	(vii)	(vi)	(v)
(d)	(iii)	(ii)	(i)	(iv)

23. Fill in the blanks with the help of options, given in the box.

(i) 15,	(ii) 250,	(iii) $\frac{1}{2}$,	(iv) 2,
(v) $\frac{1}{2}$,	(vi) $\frac{1000}{6}$,	(vii) 200,	
(viii) 12:30 pm,	(ix) 100,	(x) $12\frac{1}{2}$	

I. If $\frac{2}{5}$th of a work is completed in 10 days the ___ days to complete $\frac{1}{2}$ of the work.

II. If 30 dozens of eggs cost ₹ 600. Then, cost of 5 dozens of eggs is ___ .

III. If 5 men or 10 women can complete a work in same time. Then, 1 man = ___ women.

IV. If Divya travels 50 m distance in 75 steps. Then, the distance travelled in 375 steps is ___ m.

Codes

	I	II	III	IV
(a)	(x)	(ix)	(iv)	(ii)
(b)	(i)	(iii)	(iv)	(v)
(c)	(vi)	(viii)	(ix)	(x)
(d)	(xi)	(ii)	(iii)	(iv)

Chapter 08

Profit, Loss and Discount

1 Mark Questions

1. A shopkeeper sold an article at 20% profit, that means he has got 20% extra on which of the price?
(a) Cost price (b) Selling price
(c) Marked price (d) None of these

2. If selling price of an article is $\frac{5}{4}$ of its cost price and in this transaction amount of profit is ₹ 20, then CP : SP is
(a) 3 : 5 (b) 4 : 5
(c) 3 : 2 (d) 3 : 4

3. If 6 articles are sold for ₹ 1, then there is a loss of 20%. In order to gain 20%, then the number of articles sold for ₹ 1 are
(a) 2 (b) 4
(c) 6 (d) 8

4. Rohan sold a watch to Mohan at 20% gain and Mohan sold it to Sohan at a loss of 10%. If Sohan bought the watch for ₹ 216, then the price Rohan purchased it is
(a) ₹ 400 (b) ₹ 150
(c) ₹ 200 (d) ₹ 600

5. Which of following is incorrect?
(a) Gain % $= \frac{\text{Gain}}{\text{CP}} \times 100$
(b) Loss % $= \frac{\text{Loss}}{\text{CP}} \times 100$
(c) CP $= \frac{100}{(100 + \text{Loss\%})} \times \text{SP}$
(d) CP $= \frac{100}{(100 + \text{Gain\%})} \times \text{SP}$

6. A vendor purchased 40 dozen bananas for ₹ 250. Out of these, 30 bananas were rotten and could not be sold. At what rate per dozen should be sell the remaining bananas to make a profit of 20%?
(a) ₹20 (b) ₹ 15 (c) ₹8 (d) ₹2.5

7. *A* sells a bicycle to *B* at a profit of 30% and *B* sells it to *C* at a loss of 20%. If *C* pays ₹ 520 for it, then at what price did *A* buy?
(a) ₹ 450 (b) ₹ 500
(c) ₹ 600 (d) ₹ 550

8. A man buys 5 oranges in ₹ 6 and sells 6 oranges in ₹ 5. In this transaction, he experiences loss. To gain 20% profit, what should be the selling rate of each orange?
(a) ₹ 2 per orange
(b) ₹ 1 per orange
(c) ₹ 1.44 per orange
(d) None of the above

9. Equivalent discount of 20%, 10% and 10% is
(a) 40% (b) 35%
(c) 35.2% (d) 65%

10. By selling 90 ball pens for ₹ 160 a person loses 20%, then the number of ball pens sold for ₹ 96 so as to have a profit of 20% are :

(a) 36 (b) 42
(c) 18 (d) 34

11. The marked price of an article is ₹ 500. The shopkeeper gives a discount of 5% and still makes a profit of 25%. Then, how much did the article cost?

(a) ₹ 400 (b) ₹ 350
(c) ₹ 380 (d) ₹ 450

12. Two stores *A* and *B* charge ₹ 750 for a video game. This week, there is a sale offer on both the stores. The video game available at store *B* is of ₹ 600 and 25% off at store *A*. At which store, the video game is less expensive?

(a) *A* (b) *B*
(c) Same at *A* and *B* (d) None of these

13. Choose odd one from the given figures.

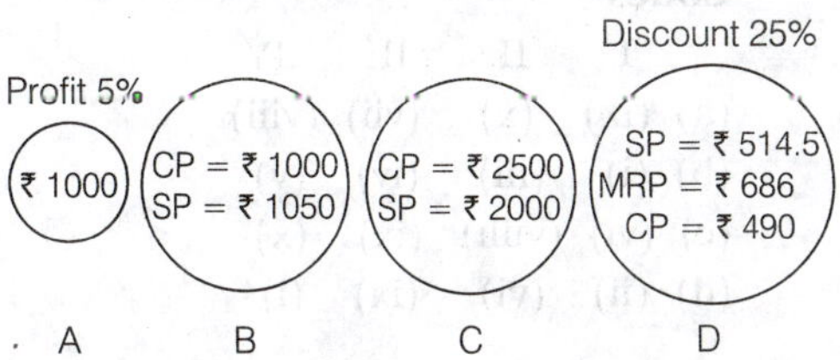

(a) A (b) B
(c) C (d) D

14. State 'T' for true or 'F' for false.

I. If selling price is less than cost price, then profit occurs.
II. Discount percent is calculated on SP.
III. On selling a fan for ₹ 810, the gain is 8%. Then, CP of fan is ₹ 750.
IV. The marked price is always fixed more than selling price.
V. CP = MP – Discount

Codes

	I	II	III	IV	V
(a)	F	F	T	T	F
(b)	T	T	T	T	F
(c)	F	T	T	T	F
(d)	T	T	T	F	T

15. A shopkeeper increase the price of an item by 20% and then allows a discount of 15%. How much has the customer to pay if the item was initially priced at ₹ 1500?

(a) ₹ 1590
(b) ₹ 1440
(c) ₹ 1530
(d) ₹ 1680

2 Marks Questions

16. A dealer sold a radio at a loss of 2.5%. Had he sold it for ₹ 100 more, he would have gained 7.5%. For what value should he sell it in order to gain $12\frac{1}{2}\%$?

(a) ₹ 1000 (b) ₹ 1125
(c) ₹ 1250 (d) ₹ 1500

17. What is more favourable for a buyer–

A discount series of 20%, 15% and 10% or a discount series of 25%, 12% and 8%?

(a) First
(b) Second
(c) Both First and Second
(d) None

18. The marked price of a pen is increased by 20% and then a discount of 20% is allowed. If marked price is not increased and discount of 20% is offered. Then, by how much per cent is the selling price changed?

(a) 25% (b) 20% (c) −20% (d) −10%

19. Match the following.

	Column I		Column II
I.	If CP = 150, loss percent = 20%, then SP =	(i)	Profit
II.	If SP = 250, profit percent = 25%, then CP =	(ii)	₹ 120
III.	If profit = 10% and loss = 10%, then (successive) resultant will be	(iii)	₹ 200
IV.	If SP > CP, then ... occurs.	(iv)	1% loss

Codes

	I	II	III	IV
(a)	(i)	(ii)	(iii)	(iv)
(b)	(ii)	(iii)	(iv)	(i)
(c)	(ii)	(iv)	(iii)	(i)
(d)	(ii)	(i)	(iii)	(iv)

20. Fill in the blanks with the help of options, given in the box.

(i) 800, (ii) 4.5, (iii) 195,
(iv) discount, (v) 2.5,
(vi) $11\frac{1}{9}$%, (vii) 1000,
(viii) 199.5, (ix) Sales tax,
(x) 10%

I. ___ is charged on the sale of an item by the government and is added to the bill amount.

II. A vendor losses the selling price of 4 oranges on selling 36 oranges. His loss % is ___ .

III. The marked price of an article when it is sold for ₹ 880 after a discount of 12%, is ___ .

IV. 5% sales tax is charged on an article marked ₹ 200 after allowing a discount of 5%, then amount payable is ___.

Codes

	I	II	III	IV
(a)	(ix)	(x)	(vii)	(viii)
(b)	(i)	(iii)	(iv)	(v)
(c)	(vi)	(viiii)	(ix)	(x)
(d)	(ii)	(vi)	(ix)	(i)

Chapter 09

Simple and Compound Interest

1 Mark Questions

1. Rohan borrows ₹ 20000 for 73 days at 10% simple interest per year from his friend Puneet for admission of his son in a school. Find the interest he has to pay to his friend after 73 days.
(a) ₹ 388 (b) ₹ 400
(c) ₹ 560 (d) ₹ 640

2. Sunil lent ₹ 12000 to his friend Akshay at 5% simple interest which amount to ₹ 18000 after a certain period of time. Find the time period.
(a) 6 yr (b) 8 yr (c) 10 yr (d) 15 yr

3. In how much time would the simple interest on a certain sum be 0.5 times of its principal at 8% per annum?
(a) 6 yr 3 months (b) 8 yr
(c) 8 yr 6 months (d) 6 yr

4. If the simple interest on a certain sum of money is $\frac{1}{4}$ th of the principal and rate of interest is equal to the time for which interest is found. Find the rate of interest on that sum of money.
(a) 5% (b) 10%
(c) 7.5% (d) 2.5%

5. Rahul borrowed some amount at the rate of 6% per annum for first 2 yr, at the rate of 9% per annum for next 3 yr at simple interest. If he pays a total interest of ₹ 11400 at the end of 9 yr, then how much amount did he borrow?
(a) ₹ 29230.8 (b) ₹ 13000
(c) ₹ 11000 (d) ₹ 14000

6. A sum is taken for 3 yr at 10% per annum. If interest is compounded after every three months, then the number of times for which interest is changed in 3 yr, is
(a) 8 (b) 12 (c) 6 (d) 9

7. If a sum of money is borrowed at 5% compound interest and paid back in two annual instalments of ₹ 882 each. Then, the sum borrowed was
(a) ₹ 1600 (b) ₹ 1640
(c) ₹ 1680 (d) ₹ 1700

8. 3 yr ago the population of a town was 160000. If it increased by 3%, 2.5% and 5%, respectively in the last three years, then the present population is
(a) 173662 (b) 177366
(c) 163662 (d) 183236

9. Anita borrowed a sum of money from Raju at the rate of 5% per annum at compound interest for 2 yr. She returned ₹ 5000 on the end of first year. At the end of second year, she returned ₹ 3820. The principal borrowed was

(a) ₹ 8000 (b) ₹ 8500
(c) ₹ 9000 (d) ₹ 7500

10. If the rate of interest be 4% per annum for first year, 5% per annum for second year and 6% per annum for third year, then the compound interest on ₹ 10000 for 3 yr is

(a) 1575 (b) 1575.20
(c) 1275 (d) 1275.20

11. The population of a village is 8000. It increases by 10% during first year and by 20% during second year. Due to malaria in third year, the population decreases by 20%. The population of village after three years is

(a) 8500 (b) 8448
(c) 8400 (d) 8800

12. What amount that Prateek will receive, if he deposits ₹ 8000 for 3 yr at 10% per annum compouned annually?

(a) ₹ 10228
(b) ₹ 12556
(c) ₹ 11205
(d) ₹ 10648

13. A certain sum doubles itself in 2 yr at r% simple interest per annum or at R% compound interest per annum. Then, we have

(a) $r < R$ (b) $r = R$
(c) $r > R$ (d) Can't say

14. Mehak and Monisha borrowed ₹ 62500 and ₹ 60000 respectively for a period of 2 yr. Mehak paid simple interest at the rate of 4% per annum, while Monisha paid compound interest at the same rate compounded annually. Who paid more interest and by how much?

(a) Mehak paid more by ₹ 104
(b) Monisha paid more by ₹ 104
(c) Both paid equal
(d) None of the above

15. State 'T' for true and 'F' for false.

I. The CI and SI on the same principal for same time period and at same rate of interest are also equal. ($t > 1$)

II. Simple interest is calculated by using the formula, $SI = P\left(1+\frac{r}{100}\right)^n$.

III. The population of a city whose growth rate is known, is calculated by using the compound interest formula.

IV. If a sum of ₹ 1000 becomes 1331 after 3 yr, then rate of interest is 10% per annum.

Codes

	I	II	III	IV
(a)	F	F	T	F
(b)	F	T	T	T
(c)	T	F	F	T
(d)	T	T	T	F

16. Find a and b, then match the following:

Column I	Column II
I. SI = CI for T is equal to	(i) 4
II. $A = P\left(1+\frac{R}{100}\right)^?$	(ii) n
III. $P = 500$, $R = 10\%$, $SI = 40$, T is equal to	(iii) 1
IV. $T = 2$ yr, if CI calculated half yearly, then n is equal to	(iv) $\frac{4}{5}$ yr

Codes

	I	II	III	IV
(a)	(i)	(ii)	(iii)	(iv)
(b)	(iii)	(ii)	(iv)	(i)
(c)	(iii)	(i)	(ii)	(iv)
(d)	(ii)	(i)	(iv)	(iii)

2 Marks Questions

17. A sum of ₹ 1550 was lent partly at 5% and partly at 8% per annum simple interest. The total amount (interest) received after three years is ₹ 300. The ratio of the money lent on 5% and that of 8% are

(a) 5 : 8
(b) 8 : 5
(c) 16 : 15
(d) 31 : 6

18. If m, n and p are the three sums of money such that n is the simple interest on m and p is the simple interest on n for the same time and at the same rate of interest. The relation among m, n and p is given by

(a) $n^2 = mp$
(b) $m^2 = np$
(c) $p^2 = nm$
(d) $p = mn$

19. The difference between compound interest and simple interest on a sum for 2 yr at 8% per annum is ₹ 768. The sum is

(a) ₹ 100000
(b) ₹110000
(c) ₹ 120000
(d) ₹170000

20. A sum of money at compound interest amounts to 3 times of itself in 3 yr. In how many years will it be 9 times of itself?

(a) 6 yr (b) 5 yr
(c) 9 yr (d) 7 yr

21. The CI on a certain sum of money for 2 yr at 10% per annum is ₹ 420.
Calculate SI on the same sum for double the time at half the rate per cent per annum.

(a) ₹ 450 (b) ₹ 400
(c) ₹ 560 (d) ₹ 360

22. Fill in the blanks with the help of options, given in the box.

(i) 40%,	(ii) 2.5%,	(iii) 4,
(iv) ≥,	(v) 2,	(vi) >,
(vii) ₹ 1000,	(viii) ₹ 10000,	(ix) 1655.06,
(x) 12155.06		

I. CI = ___, if $P = 10500$, $R = 5\%$ per annum and $T = 3$ yr.

II. Rate $= 10\%$ per annum, when compounded quarterly for 1 yr by the formula, $A = P\left(1 + \frac{r}{100}\right)^n$, $r =$ ___ .

III. Amount after n yr, compounded half-yearly is $P\left(1 + \frac{r}{\_\_\_ \times 100}\right)^{2n}$.

IV. CI is always ___ than SI for time period more than 1 yr.

Codes

	I	II	III	IV
(a)	(ix)	(ii)	(v)	(vi)
(b)	(i)	(ii)	(iv)	(v)
(c)	(vi)	(vii)	(ix)	(x)
(d)	(x)	(vii)	(iv)	(i)

Chapter 10

Algebraic Expressions

1 Mark Questions

1. Sum of $5x^2 + 3x - 8$ and $4x^2 - 5x + 6$ is

(a) $9x^2 + 8x - 2$ (b) $9x^2 - 2x - 2$

(c) $9x^2 - 8x + 2$ (d) $9x^2 - 2x + 2$

2. If $P = -2y^2 + \frac{1}{2}y - 3$ and $Q = 7y^2 - 2y + 10$, then the value of $(Q - P)$ is

(a) $5y^2 - \frac{5}{2}y + 7$ (b) $5y^2 - \frac{1}{2}y + 13$

(c) $9y^2 - \frac{5}{2}y + 13$ (d) $9y^2 - \frac{1}{2}y - 13$

3. Which of the following statements is true?

(a) $g(x) + g(y) = 2g(x)$

(b) $f(y) - f(x) = 0$

(c) $g(x) + 2g(x) = 3g(x)$

(d) All of the above

4. Which of the following is true

(a) $9x^2 + 6y + 6x^2 - 3y + 2x - 5x^2 = 10x^2 + 3y - 2x$

(b) $6x^2 + 6y + 9x^2 - 3y + 2x - 5x^2 = 10x^2 + 3y + 2x$

(c) $5x^2 + 6y + 6x^2 - 3y + 2x + 9y^2 = 10x^2 + 3y + x$

(d) $6y + 6x^2 - 3y + 2x - 9y^2 + 5x^2 = 10x^2 + 3y^2 + 2x$

5. If $A = 7xy + 5y$ and $B = 3xy$, then the value of AB is

(a) $21xy + 15xy^2$

(b) $21x^2y^2 + 15x^2y$

(c) $21x^2y^2 + 15xy^2$

(d) $21xy^2 + 15xy^2$

6. Sum of $a - b + ab$, $b + c - bc$ and $c - a - ac$ is

(a) $2c + ab - ac - bc$

(b) $2c - ab - ac - bc$

(c) $2c + ab + ac + bc$

(d) $2c - ab + ac + bc$

7. What must be added to $x^3 + x^2 + x - 1$ to get $x^4 + 2x^2 - 3x + 7$?

(a) $x^4 - x^3 + x^2 - 4x + 8$

(b) $x^3 + x^2 - 4x + 8$

(c) $x^4 - x^3 + x^2 + 4x - 8$

(d) $x^4 - x^3 - x^2 + 4x - 8$

8. The length of a rectangle is x m while its breadth is 5 less than twice its length. Write an expression to represent the perimeter of the rectangle.

(a) $6x - 10$ (b) $6x - 5$

(c) $3x + 5$ (d) $3x - 10$

9. The breadth of a rectangle is 4 less than its length while its length is x unit. Write an expression to represent the area of the rectangle.

(a) x^2+4x

(b) x^2-4x

(c) x^2+4

(d) x^2-4

10. Product of (x^2+3x+5) and (x^2-1) is

(a) $x^4+3x^3-4x^2-3x-5$

(b) $x^4+3x^3+4x^2-3x-5$

(c) $x^4+3x^3+4x^2+3x-5$

(d) x^4+x^3+x+5

11. $\left(\frac{x}{2}-\frac{3y}{4}\right)\left(\frac{5x}{4}-\frac{y}{2}\right)=?$

(a) $\frac{5x^2}{8}-\frac{19xy}{16}+\frac{3y^2}{8}$

(b) $\frac{5x^2}{8}+\frac{19xy}{16}+\frac{3y^2}{4}$

(c) $\frac{5x^2}{8}-\frac{11xy}{16}+\frac{3y^2}{4}$

(d) $\frac{5x^2}{8}+\frac{11xy}{16}+\frac{3y^2}{4}$

12. The area of rectangle is $x^2+7x+12$. If its length is $(x+3)$, then the breadth will be (when $x=2$)

(a) 6 (b) 8

(c) 12 (d) 2

13. If $\frac{6\times6-1.5\times1.5}{4.5}=a+b$, then the value of a

(a) 5 (b) 8

(c) 10 (d) 6

14. What will be the value of $n^4-10n^3+36n^2-49n+24$, if $n=1$.

(a) 21 (b) 2

(c) 1 (d) 22

15. Which of following is correct for $m=3, n=1$.

(a) $6m^2-6mn-6m+18=0$

(b) $6m^2-9mn-3m-20=-2$

(c) $9m^2-18mn-6n+2=6$

(d) $8m^2-6mn+6m+7=-4$

16. The value of expression $\frac{2x^3-12x^2+16x}{(x-2)(x-4)}$ is

(a) 2 (b) $\frac{x}{2}$

(c) $2x$ (d) $2x^2$

17. The value of the product $\left(2+\frac{4}{x}\right)\left(10-\frac{15}{x}+\frac{25}{x^2}\right)$ at $x=1$ is

(a) 150 (b) 120

(c) 200 (d) 240

18. The perimeter of a triangle is $8p^2-9p+9$ and two of its sides are $2p^2-3p+1$ and $5p^2-p+4$. Then, third side of the triangle is

(a) $2p^2-6p+5$

(b) p^2-5p+4

(c) $3p^2-2p+1$

(d) $4p^2+3p+6$

19. The value of $8p^3+6x^2+9pq-8pqx$, if $x=pq$ and $p=q=4$.

(a) 256 (b) 512

(c) 296 (d) 144

20. The value of expression $\frac{6p^3-36p^2+48p}{(p-2)(p-4)}$ at $p=8$ is

(a) 36 (b) 72

(c) 48 (d) 216

2 Marks Questions

21. If $2x+3y=6\sqrt{3}$ and $2x-3y=6$, then the value of x and y are respectively

(a) $x=\frac{1}{2}(\sqrt{3}+1), y=\sqrt{3}+1$

(b) $x=\frac{3}{2}(\sqrt{3}+1), y=\sqrt{3}-1$

(c) $x=\frac{5}{2}(\sqrt{3}-1), y=\sqrt{3}+1$

(d) $x=\frac{3}{2}(\sqrt{3}-1), y=2\sqrt{3}-3$

22. If $2x+3y=23$ and $2x-3y=5$, then the value of expression $\frac{2x^2+3x+1}{4y^2-9y+31}$ is equal to

(a) 3 (b) 6 (c) 12 (d) 9

23. What should be added to the product of (x^2+xy-y^2) and (x^2-xy+y^2) to get x^2y^2?

(a) $2xy-x^4-2xy^3+y^4$

(b) $2x^2y^2-x^4-2xy^3+y^4$

(c) $2x^2y^2-x^3-2x^3y+y^2$

(d) $4xy^2-2x+4y^7$

24. Fill in the blanks with the help of options given in the box.

(i) 36, (ii) $2xy$, (iii) $x(a+b)$, (iv) $(a+b)$, (v) $15xy$, (vi) 0, (vii) 81, (viii) 21, (ix) 4

I. $(x-y)\times(3x+5y)=3x^2+$ .... $-5y^2$.

II. $(x+a)(x+b)=x^2+$ .... $+ab$.

III. If $a=b=c$, then $a^2+b^2+c^2-ab-bc-ca$ is ....

IV. If $y=-2$ then $3y(2y-7)-3(y-4)-63=$ ....

V. Coefficient of z^2 in the expression $x^2+4xz+4z^2$ is ....

Codes

	I	II	III	IV	V
(a)	(ii)	(iii)	(vi)	(viii)	(ix)
(b)	(i)	(ii)	(iii)	(iv)	(v)
(c)	(v)	(vii)	(viii)	(ix)	(vi)
(d)	(i)	(ii)	(ix)	(vi)	(iii)

25. State 'T' for true or 'F' for false.

I. The sum of $(2x+y)^2$ and $(6x^2+3y^2-4xy)$ is $10x^2+4y^2$.

II. On dividing $\frac{x}{4}$ by $\frac{4}{x}$, then the quotient is 16.

III. $(5x-63)\div 9=5x-7$.

IV. The value of p for $64^2-56^2=120p$, is 8.

Codes

	I	II	III	IV
(a)	T	F	F	T
(b)	T	T	T	F
(c)	T	T	F	T
(d)	F	F	T	T

26. Match the following.

Column I	Column II
I. sum of $5m(3-m)$ and $(6m^2-13m)$	(i) $14m^3+12m^2-28m+10$
II. $(x+a)(x+b)$ is equal to, if $a=2, b=3$	(ii) x^2+5x+6
III. 34×26 can be written in the form of	(iii) $(x+b)(x-b)$
IV. $[4m(3m^2+5m-7)+2(m^3-4m^2+5)]$ is equal to	(iv) m^2+2m

Codes

	I	II	III	IV
(a)	(i)	(ii)	(iii)	(iv)
(b)	(iv)	(ii)	(iii)	(i)
(c)	(iv)	(iii)	(ii)	(i)
(d)	(i)	(iii)	(ii)	(iv)

Chapter

11

Factorisation of Algebraic Expressions

1 Mark Questions

1. Factors of $17ab - 68ab^2$.

(a) $17ab(1-4b)$ (b) $17a^2b(1-4b)$

(c) $17ab(1+4b)$ (d) $17ab(4b-1)$

2. If we factorise $xy - pq + qy - px$. The factors, thus obtained are

(a) $(y-p)(x+q)$ (b) $(y-p)(x-q)$

(c) $(y+p)(x+q)$ (d) $(y+p)(x-q)$

3. The factor of $6 - y - 2y^2$ is

(a) $y+2$ (b) $y-3$

(c) $-2y+3$ (d) Both (a) and (c)

4. In factorisation, we use various techniques to do so. One of the techniques is illustrated here.

Step I $x^2 - 13x + 42$

Step II $x^2 - 7x - 6x + 42$

Step III $x^2 - 13x + 42 + 13 - 13$

Step IV $x(x-7) - 6(x-7)$

Step V Factors are $(x-6)$ and $(x-7)$.

Which of the following steps shown above is wrong?

(a) I (b) II (c) IV (d) III

5. If cost of 1 shirt is ₹ $(2x^2 - 4x - 10)$, then cost of $(x+2)$ shirts is

(a) $x^3 - 8x^2 + 8x - 3$ (b) $2x^3 + 18x - 20$

(c) $2x^3 - 18x - 20$ (d) None of these

6. After factorising $10x^2 + 21x + 9$, we see that the factors are in the form of $(2x+3)(5x+3)$. So, the factors of 1219 can be written as, (x is a natural number)

(a) 53×33 (b) 23×53

(c) 33×23 (d) None of these

7. After factorising $2x^2 - \frac{5}{6}x + \frac{1}{12}$, the factors can be written in the form of

(a) $\left(\frac{x}{2} - \frac{1}{12}\right)(4x-1)$ (b) $\left(\frac{x}{12} - 1\right)(4x+2)$

(c) $\left(\frac{x}{2} + \frac{1}{12}\right)\left(12 + \frac{4}{x}\right)$ (d) $\left(\frac{x}{2} - \frac{1}{12}\right)(4x+6)$

8. If $6x^2 + 19x + 8 = A(x+3) + 5$, then the value of A is

(a) $(6x+3)$ (b) $(6x+1)$

(c) $(2+3x)$ (d) $(6x-1)$

9. One of the factors of $(x^2 - 5x)(x^2 - 5x - 20) + 84$ is given by

(a) $(x^2 + 2)$ (b) $(x + 3)$

(c) $(x - 7)$ (d) $(x - 5)$

10. One of the factors of $x^2 + \frac{1}{x^2} + 2 - 2x - \frac{2}{x}$ is given by

(a) $x - \frac{1}{x}$ (b) $x + \frac{1}{x} - 1$

(c) $x + \frac{1}{x} - 2$ (d) $x^2 + \frac{1}{x^2}$

11. If $x^8 - x^4 - 72 = (x^4 - A)(x^4 + B)$, then the value of A and B is given by

(a) $A = -9, B = 8$ (b) $A = 9, B = -8$

(c) $A = 3, B = 8$ (d) $A = 9, B = 8$

12. Which method is used in the factorisation shown below?

(i) $x^2 + 8x + 16$

(ii) $(x)^2 + (4)^2 + 2 \cdot x \cdot 4$

(iii) $(x + 4)^2$; $(a + b)^2 = a^2 + b^2 + 2ab$

(iv) $(x + 4)(x + 4)$

(a) Splitting middle term

(b) Algebraic identity

(c) Both (a) and (b)

(d) None of the above

13. If $y^2 + 18y + 65 = ay^2 + 2by + 65$. Then, the value of $\frac{(a + b)}{(a - b)}$ is

(a) $\frac{19}{18}$ (b) $-\frac{5}{4}$ (c) $\frac{4}{5}$ (d) Can't say

14. If $(x^3y^3 + x^2y^3 - xy^4 + xy) \div xy$ and quotient is factorised, then factors of quotient are

(a) $(x + 1)$ (b) $(y - 1)$

(c) Can't factorise (d) $x^2 - y^2$

15. Simplify the given expression $[(5x - 3)^2 - (5x - 3) - 20] \div (5x - 8)$

(a) $5x + 3$ (b) $5x - 3$ (c) $5x + 8$ (d) $5x + 1$

2 Marks Questions

16. Choose the odd one from the given algebraic expressions.

(A) $x^2 - 4x + 4$ (B) $x^2 - 5x + 6$

(C) $x^2 - 9x + 18$ (D) $3x^2 - 24x + 36$

(a) A (b) B (c) C (d) D

17. If the area of square is equal to the area of rectangle given below. Find the value of x.

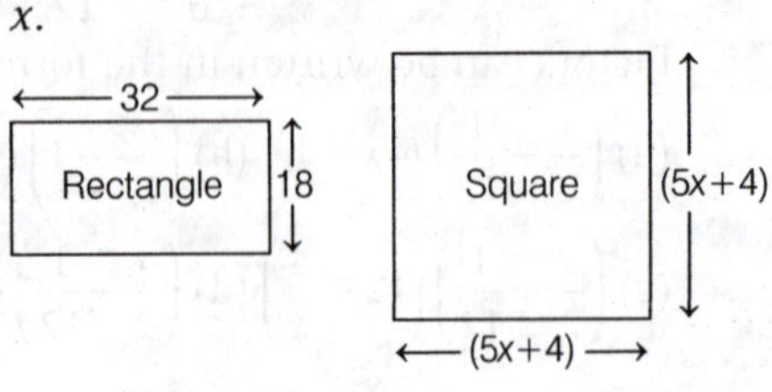

(a) 4 (b) 5 (c) $\frac{25}{9}$ (d) $\frac{16}{7}$

18. Simplified value of

$$\frac{6 \times 1.5 \times 1.5 + 1.5 \times 18 + 1.5 + 3}{2 \times 1.5 \times 1.5 - 8 \times 1.5 + 5 \times 1.5 - 20}$$

(a) $4\frac{1}{4}$ (b) $2\frac{1}{4}$ (c) $11\frac{1}{4}$ (d) $7\frac{1}{4}$

19. Fill in the blanks with the help of options, given in the box.

(i) $(2x + 3)$, (ii) $(2x - 3)$, (iii) 4, (iv) 2, (v) $(x + 4)$, (vi) $(x - 4)$, (vii) 9, (viii) 7, (ix) 12

I. $8x^2 - 18x + 9 = (4x - 3) \times$ ....

II. If $x^2 - 12 - x = A \times (x + 3)$, then $A =$ ....

III. If the area of a square is 625 cm^2 and its side is $(7x - 24)$ cm, then $x =$ ....

IV. $x^2 + 10x + 16 = (x + 8)(x + p)$ then $p =$ ....

Codes

	I	II	III	IV
(a)	(i)	(iii)	(vii)	(iii)
(b)	(ii)	(vi)	(viii)	(iv)
(c)	(i)	(vi)	(viii)	(ix)
(d)	(ii)	(vi)	(ix)	(iii)

Chapter 12

Linear Equations in One Variable

1 Mark Questions

1. The highest power of a variable in linear equation of one variable is
   (a) 1 (b) 2
   (c) 3 (d) any number

2. Which of the following is a linear expression?
   (a) $x^2 + 3$ (b) $z + z^2$
   (c) 7 (d) $1 + x$

3. Which of the following is a linear equation in one variable?
   (a) $(2x - 2)^2 = 4x^2 + 4x - 4$
   (b) $(3x - 4)^2 = 3x - 3x^2 + 3$
   (c) $x^2 = 2x - 2$
   (d) All of the above

4. The correct value of x in the equation $\frac{3x-1}{3x+1} = \frac{2x+3}{2x-1}$
   (a) $\frac{1}{8}$ (b) $\frac{-1}{8}$ (c) $\frac{8}{3}$ (d) $\frac{-8}{3}$

5. Simplest form of the equation $\frac{6x+1}{3} + 1 = \frac{x-3}{6}$ is given by
   (a) $11x - 3 = 8$ (b) $11x + 8 = 3$
   (c) $11x + 8 = -3$ (d) $3x + 11 = 8$

6. The solution of the linear equation $3x + 2(x+5) = 75$ is
   (a) $x = 13$
   (b) $y = 8$
   (c) $x = 18$
   (d) $y = 15$

7. The solution of which of the following equations is neither an odd nor an even?
   (a) $3y + 2 = 4y + 2$
   (b) $4z - 18 = 6$
   (c) $3x + 7 = 5x + 3$
   (d) $5y - 8 = y + 4$

8. $x = -2$ is the solution of the equation
   (a) $6x - 3 = 3x - 5$
   (b) $x - 3 = x + 4$
   (c) $5x - 3 = 3x - 7$
   (d) $7x - 6 = 6x - 5$

9. For what value of a, the expression $\frac{a-8}{5}$ is equal to $\frac{a-6}{3}$?
   (a) 7
   (b) 3
   (c) 12
   (d) 5

10. The value of x in the given linear equation in one variable is

$$\frac{x}{3}-\frac{1}{4}\left(x-\frac{1}{2}\right)=\frac{1}{8}(x+1)+\frac{1}{12}$$

(a) 2 (b) −2
(c) 12 (d) 16

11. What is the value of x, if $\frac{x+23}{5}+5(x-3)=\frac{x+3}{2}+3x$?

(a) 10 (b) 8
(c) 12 (d) 7

12. If $0.18(5y-4)=0.5y+0.8$, then the value of y is

(a) 5.8
(b) 3.26
(c) 3.86
(d) 3.8

13. Given $\frac{(x^2-5x+6)}{(x^2-7x+12)}=\frac{(x^2-x-6)}{(x^2+7x+10)}$, then value of x is

(a) 2.40
(b) −2.0
(c) 2.20
(d) 2.30

14. Solution for $\frac{3t-2}{4}-\frac{2t+3}{3}=\frac{2}{3}-t$

(a) $t=4$
(b) $t=1.5$
(c) $t=2$
(d) $t=3$

15. If $0.3y+0.4=0.28y+1.16$, then the value of $\frac{2y+24}{0.5y+101}$

(a) $\frac{1}{6}$ (b) $\frac{5}{6}$
(c) $-\frac{5}{6}$ (d) $-\frac{1}{6}$

16. Given $\frac{6x^2+13x-4}{2x+5}=\frac{12x^2+5x-2}{4x+3}$, then the value of $\frac{2x^2+3x+2}{5x+7}$.

(a) $-\frac{7}{12}$
(b) $\frac{7}{12}$
(c) $\frac{3}{14}$
(d) $-\frac{5}{7}$

17. If $\frac{2}{5}(4x-1)-\left[4x-\left(\frac{1-3x}{2}\right)\right]=\frac{x-7}{2}$, then the value of x is

(a) 0 (b) $\frac{9}{11}$
(c) $\frac{2}{11}$ (d) −1

18. State 'T' for true or 'F' for false.

I. x^2+2 is a linear equation in one variable.
II. The terms linear equation and linear expression are same.
III. If x is an odd number, then the next even number is $(2x+1)$.
IV. If both sides of an equation is to be divided by the same number (non-zero), then there is a change in equality.
V. 1 is the solution of $\frac{x}{2}-\frac{4}{5}+\frac{x}{5}+\frac{3x}{10}=\frac{1}{5}$.

Codes

	I	II	III	IV	V
(a)	T	F	T	F	T
(b)	T	T	T	T	T
(c)	F	F	F	F	T
(d)	F	T	F	F	F

2 Marks Questions

19. Choose the odd one from the given series.

(a) $\frac{3x-5}{6}=\frac{x}{3}$

(b) $\frac{z}{3}-\frac{1}{3}=\frac{4}{3}$

(c) $6y+7=3y+22$

(d) $\frac{7y-1}{4}=\frac{10}{3}$

20. Which of the following equations having $x=12$, as its solution?

(a) $\frac{x}{3}-\frac{x}{2}=8$

(b) $\frac{x}{3}-\frac{x}{4}=16$

(c) $\frac{x}{2}+\frac{x}{3}-\frac{x}{4}=7$

(d) $\frac{2x}{3}=\frac{8}{12}-\frac{0.25}{3}$

21. Which of the following equations having $t=-2$, as its solution?

(a) $2(t-2)=5(2t+2)$

(b) $3(t-3)=5(2t+1)$

(c) $3t-9=10t+3$

(d) $8(t-5)=3(2t+2)$

22. Which of the following equations is satisfied for $f=0.6$

(a) $0.25(4f-3)=0.05(10f-6)$

(b) $0.05(4f-3)=0.25(10f-3)$

(c) $0.25(4f-3)=0.25(10f-9)$

(d) $0.25(4f-3)=0.05(10f-9)$

23. Which of the following equations having $x=9$, as its solution?

(a) $\frac{2}{x+3}\frac{4}{x-3}=\frac{6}{x+3}$

(b) $\frac{3}{x-9}+\frac{2}{x-9}=\frac{6}{x-9}$

(c) $\frac{2}{x+3}-\frac{4}{x-3}=\frac{-6}{x+3}$

(d) $\frac{2}{x+3}+\frac{4}{x-3}=\frac{-6}{x+3}$

24. Fill in the blanks with the help of options, given in the box.

(i) 10 (ii) 8 (iii) –19 (iv) 6 (v) –21
(vi) 14 (vii) 7 (viii) 24 (ix) 18

I. If $2(y+3)+3(y+1)=4(2y-3)+3$, then $y=$ ....

II. For $x=-5$, $5x+\frac{7}{2}=\frac{3}{2}x-$ ....

III. If $\frac{2}{5x}-\frac{5}{3x}=\frac{1}{15}$, then $x=$ ....

IV. If $\frac{y-1}{3}-\frac{y-2}{4}=1$, then $y=$ ....

Codes

	I	II	III	IV
(a)	(i)	(ii)	(iii)	(iv)
(b)	(iv)	(vi)	(iii)	(i)
(c)	(ix)	(viii)	(vii)	(v)
(d)	(i)	(vi)	(iii)	(i)

25. Match the following:

	Column I	Column II
I.	If $8x-5-3x=6x-4x+4$, then x is	(i) –1
II.	Number of solution for a linear equation in one variable is	(ii) 3
III.	If x is three times the smallest prime number and also five less than the smallest two-digit prime number, then x is	(iii) 1
IV.	If $\frac{5}{y}+7=\frac{2}{y}+4$, then y is	(iv) 6

Codes

	I	II	III	IV
(a)	(i)	(ii)	(iii)	(iv)
(b)	(ii)	(iii)	(iv)	(i)
(c)	(ii)	(iv)	(iii)	(i)
(d)	(iii)	(ii)	(i)	(iv)

Chapter

13

Geometry

1 Mark Questions

1. Find the distance between the centre and chord of length 16 cm, where diameter of circle is 20 cm.

(a) 4 cm (b) 8 cm

(c) 6 cm (d) 10 cm

2. In the following figure, x is equal to

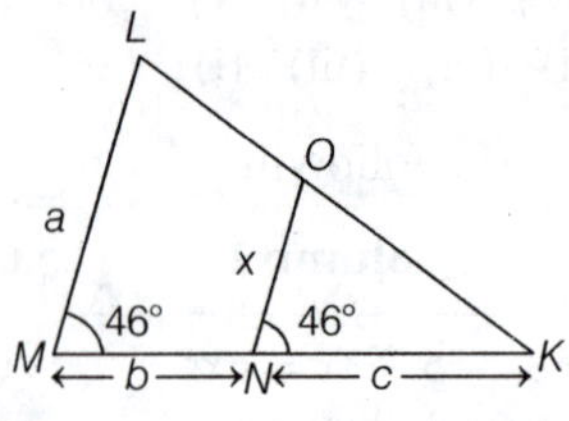

(a) $\frac{ab}{a+c}$ (b) $\frac{ac}{a+b}$

(c) $\frac{ac}{b+c}$ (d) $\frac{ab}{b+c}$

3. $\angle A$ and $\angle B$ are complementary and the measure of $\angle A$ is twice the measure of $\angle B$. Find the measures of $\angle A$ and $\angle B$.

(a) 60° and 30° (b) 45° and 45°

(c) 30° and 60° (d) 20° and 70°

4. In the given trapezium, the value of x is

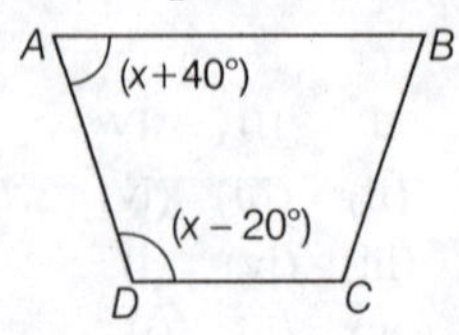

(a) 80° (b) 120° (c) 60° (d) 90°

5. The value of x in the given figure of a parallelogram is

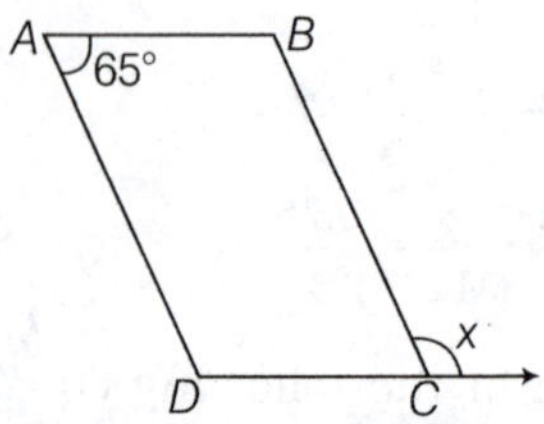

(a) 65° (b) 115°

(c) 135° (d) 25°

6. In an isosceles triangle, one of the equal angle is 54°. Find the all three angle?

(a) 54°, 54°, 72° (b) 54°, 64°, 62°

(c) 45°, 90°, 45° (d) 54°, 56°, 70°

7. The adjacent angles of a parallelogram are $(2x-4)°$ and $(3x-1)°$. The measures of all angles of parallelogram are

(a) 70°, 110°, 70°, 110°

(b) 80°, 100°, 100°, 80°

(c) 60°, 120°, 60°, 120°

(d) None of the above

8. If the measures of two adjacent angles of a parallelogram are in the ratio 7 : 2, then the measures of all the angles of parallelogram are

(a) 40°, 100°, 80°, 140°

(b) 140°, 40°, 140°, 40°

(c) 135°, 45°, 135°, 45°

(d) 120°, 60°, 60°, 120°

9. The length of diagonals of a rhombus are 10 cm and 24 cm respectively. What is the length of each of its sides?

(a) 20 cm (b) 13 cm (c) 26 cm (d) 16 cm

10. In following figure $ABCD$ is a rectangle. If $\angle COD = 162 - 3x$ and $\angle OAB = 2x$, then the value of x is equal to

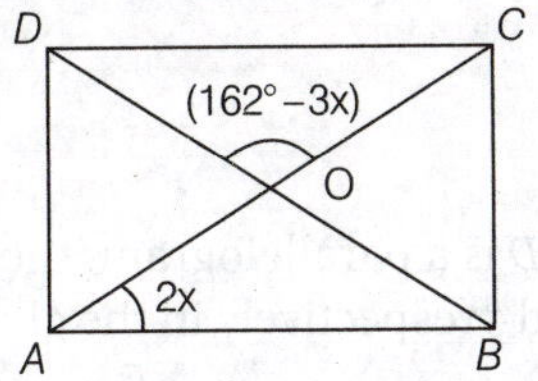

(a) 54° (b) 36° (c) 24° (d) 18°

11. In given figure $ABCD$ is a rhombus and if $\angle DAB = 2x + 15°$ and $\angle DCB = 3x - 30°$, then the value of $\angle BDC$ is equal to

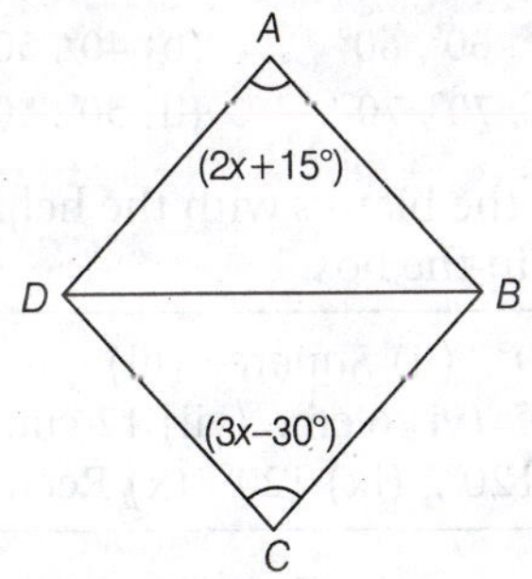

(a) 45° (b) 35° (c) 37.5° (d) 42.5°

12. In the given figure, QA and PB are perpendicular to AB. If $AO = 10$ cm, $BO = 6$ cm and $PB = 9$ cm, then the value of AQ is

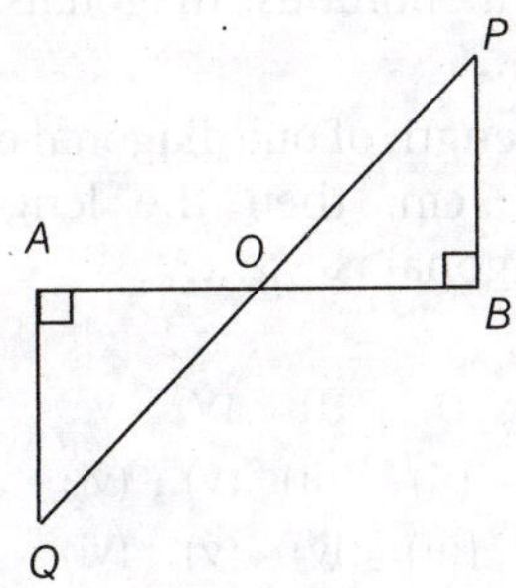

(a) 5 cm (b) 25 cm (c) 15 cm (d) 20 cm

13. Given figure is rhombus and $\angle OBA$ is 36°, then the value of $\angle x$ is

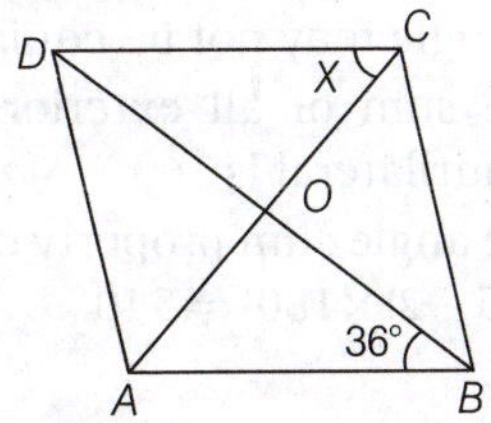

(a) 44°

(b) 54°

(c) 114°

(d) 56°

14. Find x, if ΔABC is a right triangle with $\angle B = 90°$.

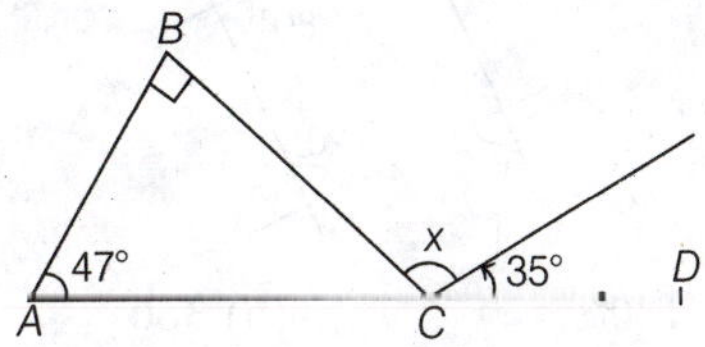

(a) 92°

(b) 102°

(c) 72°

(d) 84°

15. Match the following:

Column I	Column II
I. Rectangle	(i) All sides are equal.
II. Square	(ii) Opposite sides are equal and all angles are 90°.
III. Rhombus	(iii) All sides are equal and all angles are 90°.
IV. Trapezium	(iv) One pair of opposite sides are parallel.

Codes

	I	II	III	IV
(a)	(i)	(ii)	(iii)	(iv)
(b)	(ii)	(iii)	(i)	(iv)
(c)	(ii)	(i)	(iii)	(iv)
(d)	(iv)	(iii)	(ii)	(i)

16. State 'T' for true or 'F' for false.

I. A triangle which is an equilateral triangle may not be equiangular.

II. The sum of all exterior angles of a quadrilateral is 360°.

III. The angle sum property of a pentagon is $(5-2)\times 180° = 540°$.

IV. The sum of all interior angles of n-sided polygon is $(2n-4)$ right angles.

Codes

	I	II	III	IV
(a)	F	T	T	T
(b)	F	T	F	F
(c)	T	T	T	F
(d)	T	T	F	F

2 Marks Questions

17. In the given figure, the value of $x+y+z+w$ is

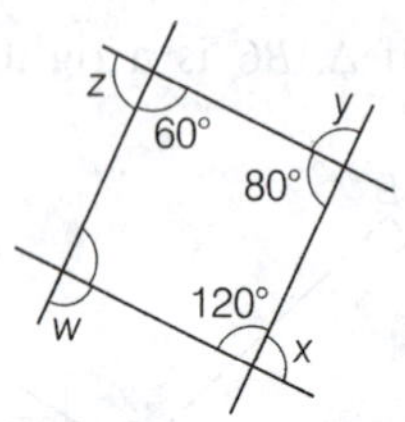

(a) 180° (b) 360°
(c) 3π (d) 120°

18. In the parallelogram *PQRS*, *O* is the mid-point of *SQ*. Then, the ratio of $\angle S$ and $\angle R$ is

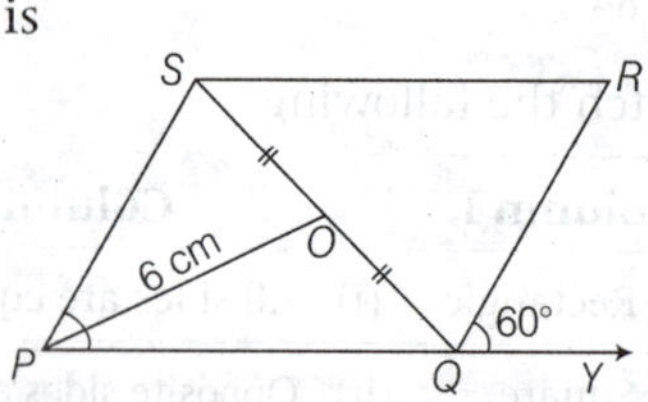

(a) 1 : 2 (b) 2 : 1 (c) 1 : 3 (d) 3 : 1

19. *PQRS* is a rectangle. If the perpendicular *ST* from *S* on *PR* divides $\angle S$ in the ratio 2 : 3, then the measure of $\angle TPQ$ is

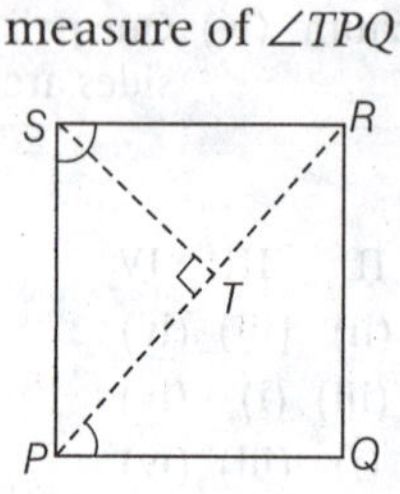

(a) 54° (b) 36°
(c) 90° (d) 18°

20. If *ABCD* is a parallelogram, then the angles *x*, *y* and *z* respectively in the given figure are

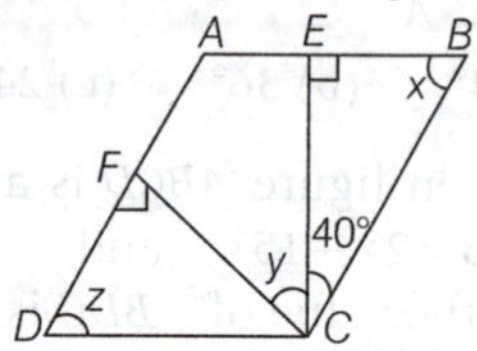

(a) 60°, 60°, 60° (b) 40°, 50°, 60°
(c) 60°, 70°, 70° (d) 50°, 50°, 50°

21. Fill in the blanks with the help of options, given in the box.

(i) 360°, (ii) Square, (iii) 60°, (iv) 12, (v) 90°, (vi) 6 cm, (vii) 12 cm, (viii) 120°, (ix) 120°, (x) Rectangle

I. Sum of the interior angles of Quadrilateral ....

II. .... is a regular quadrilateral.

III. In an equilateral triangle, each angle is ....

IV. In a rhombus, diagonals intersect at ....

V. If length of one diagonal of a rectangle is 6 cm, then the length of other diagonal is ....

Codes

	I	II	III	IV	V
(a)	(i)	(ii)	(iii)	(v)	(vi)
(b)	(ii)	(iii)	(iv)	(v)	(vi)
(c)	(vii)	(viii)	(ix)	(x)	(i)
(d)	(iv)	(v)	(vi)	(vii)	(i)

Chapter

14

Area and Perimeter

1 Mark Questions

1. From a circular sheet of radius 14 cm, a circle of radius 5 cm is cut out. Calculate the area of the remaining sheet after the smaller circle is removed.

(a) $153\pi\ cm^2$ (b) $167\pi\ cm^2$

(c) $171\pi\ cm^2$ (d) $176\pi\ cm^2$

2. A copper wire of length 132 cm is to be bent into a square and a circle. Which will have a larger area?

(a) Square (b) Circle

(c) Both has equal area

(d) None of the above

3. If the side of a square is tripled then how much time its area becomes?

(a) Double (b) Tripled

(c) Four times (d) Nine times

4. If the diagonals of a rhombus are 24 cm and 10 cm, find the perimeter of the rhombus.

(a) 26 cm (b) 48 cm

(c) 50 cm (d) 52 cm

5. The length and breadth of a rectangle are 23 cm and 12 cm respectively. Find its perimeter if the length and breadth are doubled.

(a) 120 cm (b) 140 cm

(c) 126 cm (d) 156 cm

6. A square and a rectangle have the same perimeter. Calculate the area of the rectangle if the side of the square is 35 cm and the length of the rectangle is 25 cm.

(a) $1125\ cm^2$ (b) $1250\ cm^2$

(c) $1000\ cm^2$ (d) $1450\ cm^2$

7. The volume of a wall, 5 times as high as it is breadth and 8 times as long as it is high is $18225\ m^3$. The breadth of the wall is

(a) 32.5 m (b) 5 m

(c) 4.5 m (d) 3.5 m

8. The dimensions of a cuboid are in the ratio of $1:2:3$ and its total surface area is $132\ m^2$. Find its dimensions.

(a) 12 m, 24 m, 36 m (b) 8 m, 16 m, 24 m

(c) 6 m, 12 m, 18 m (d) 7 m, 14 m, 21 m

9. Three cubes with sides in the ratio $3:4:5$ are melted to form a single cube whose diagonal is $12\sqrt{3}$ cm. Then, the sides of the cubes are

(a) 6 cm, 8 cm, 10 cm

(b) 3 cm, 4 cm, 5 cm

(c) 9 cm, 12 cm, 15 cm

(d) 12 cm, 16 cm, 20 cm

10. A cube having each sides of unit length is cut into two parts by a plane through two diagonals of two opposite faces. Then, the total suface area of each of these parts?

(a) $3+\sqrt{2}$ sq. units (b) $2+\sqrt{3}$ sq. units

(c) $3\sqrt{2}$ sq. units (d) 3 sq. units

11. Find the area of a rhombus whose one side measures 5 cm and one diagonal as 8 cm.

(a) 22 cm^2 (b) 24 cm^2
(c) 32 cm^2 (d) 40 cm^2

12. The area of a side of a box is 120 sq. cm. The area of the other side of the box is 72 sq. cm. If the area of upper surface of the box is 60 sq. cm, then the volume of the box is

(a) 259200 cm^3 (b) 84000 cm^3
(c) 86400 cm^3 (d) 720 cm^3

13. The length of a hall is 20 m and width 16 m. The sum of the areas of the floor and the flat roof is equal to the sum of the areas of the four walls. Find the volume of the hall?

(a) 2844.44 m^3 (b) 2799.99 m^3
(c) 2475.75 m^3 (d) 2933.33 m^3

14. A cuboidal box of dimensions 4 m $\times$ 3 m $\times$ 2 m is to be painted except its bottom. Calculate how much area of the box has to the painted.

(a) 21 m^2 (b) 24 m^2 (c) 36 m^2 (d) 40 m^2

15. Two cubes are joined end to end. Find the volume of the resulting cuboid, if each side of the cube is 9 cm.

(a) 1458 cm^3 (b) 1676 cm^3
(c) 1274 cm^3 (d) 1384 cm^3

16. A closed metallic cylindrical box is 1.25 m high and it has a base whose radius is 35 cm. If the sheet of metal costs ₹ 80/m^2. Find the cost of the material used in the box.

(a) ₹ 291.60 (b) ₹ 352.50
(c) ₹ 281.60 (d) ₹ 301.60

17. 160 m^3 of water is to be used to irrigate a rectangular field whose area is 800 m^2. What will be the height of the water level (in cm) in the field?

(a) 20 cm (b) 25 cm
(c) 26 cm (d) 18 cm

18. How many bricks each 24 cm by 15 cm by 12 cm, are required for a wall 36 m long, 4 m high and 30 cm thick?

(a) 12480 (b) 13658
(c) 10000 (d) 8568

19. Three metal cubes of sides 6 cm, 8 cm and 10 cm are melted and recast into a big cube. Find its total surface area.

(a) 832 cm^2 (b) 864 cm^2
(c) 1254 cm^2 (d) 784 cm^2

2 Marks Questions

20. A rectangular metal sheet of length 50 cm and breadth 22 cm is folded along its length to form a cylinder. Find its volume.

(a) 1956 cm^3 (b) 1925 cm^3
(c) 1853 cm^3 (d) 1986 cm^3

21. How many cubic metres of earth must be dug out to since a well is 16 m deep and which has a radius of 3.5 m ? If the earth taken out is spread over a rectangular plot of dimensions 22 m $\times$ 7 m. What is the height of the platform so formed?

(a) 3.5 cm (b) 5 m
(c) 4 m (d) 4.5 cm

22. An iron pipe is 21 cm long and its exterior diameter is 8 cm. If the thickness of the pipe is 1 cm and iron weighs 8 g/cm^3. Find the weight of the pipe.

(a) 3.696 kg (b) 3.882 kg
(c) 4.683 kg (d) 4.375 kg

23. An open rectangular cistern when measured outside is 1.35 m long, 1.08 m broad and 90 cm depth and is made of iron which is 2.5 cm thick. Find the capacity of the cistern.

(a) 143525 cm^3 (b) 372435 cm^3
(c) 140575 cm^3 (d) 176237 cm^3

Chapter 15

Data Handling

1 Mark Questions

Directions (Q. Nos. 1-3) *The following pie-chart gives the marks scored in an examination by a student in Hindi, English, Mathematics, Social Science and Science.*

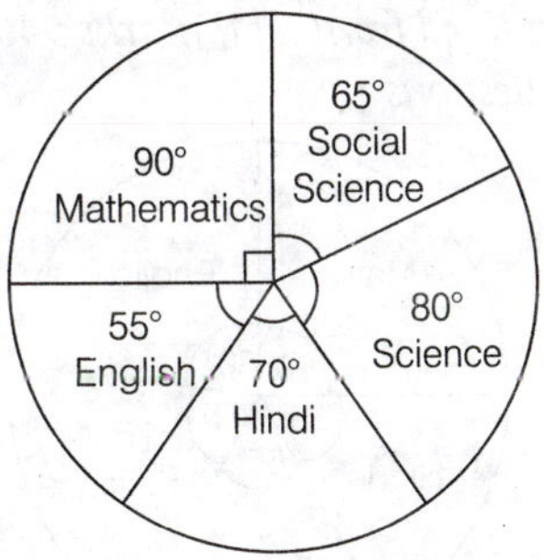

1. In which subject did the student score 105 marks? Given if the total marks obtain by the students were 540.
   (a) Science (b) Hindi
   (c) English (d) Social Science

2. How many more marks were obtained by the student in Mathematics than in Hindi? Given that if total marks obtained by the student were 540.
   (a) 105 (b) 65 (c) 30 (d) 75

3. How many more marks were obtained in the sum of the marks in Social Science and Mathematics that sum of obtained marks in Science and Hindi where total marks obtained by student were 540.
   (a) 97.5 (b) 120 (c) 7.5 (d) 37.5

4. In a class of 19 students, seven boys failed in a test. Those who passed score 12, 15, 17, 15, 16, 15, 19, 19, 17, 18, 18 and 19 marks. The median score of the 19 students in the class is
   (a) 15 (b) 16 (c) 17 (d) 18

5. The pie-chart given below shows the expenses incurred and saving by a family in a month. What is the percentage of expenses incurred on account of recreation?

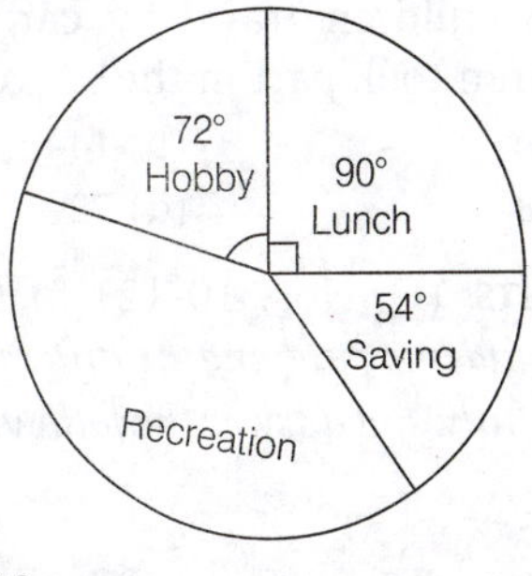

   (a) $\frac{800}{17}\%$ (b) 20%
   (c) 35% (d) 40%

6. The mean weight of the students in a certain class is 60 kg. The mean weight of the boys from the class is 70 kg and that of the girl is 55 kg. What is the ratio of the number of boys to that of girls?
   (a) 2 : 1 (b) 1 : 2
   (c) 1 : 4 (d) 4 : 1

Directions (Q. Nos. 7-9) *The given pie chart shows the result of a survey carried out to find modes of travel used by children to go to school. Study the pie chart and answer the following questions :*

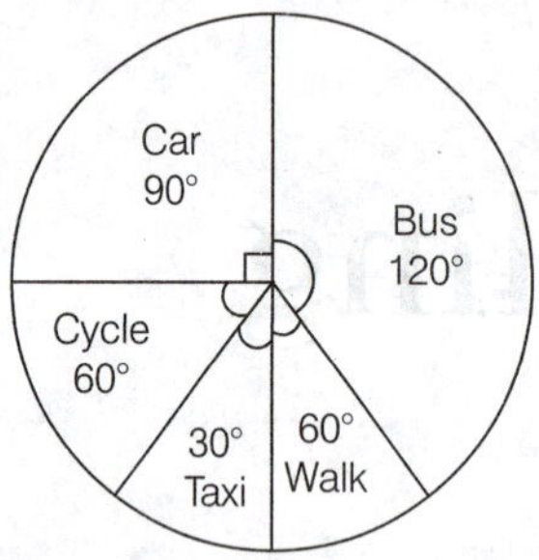

7. What is the most common mode of transport?

(a) Car (b) Bus
(c) Cycle (d) Walk

8. What fraction of children travelled by each of the mode car and cycle?

(a) $\frac{1}{4}$ and $\frac{1}{6}$ (b) $\frac{1}{12}$ and $\frac{1}{6}$
(c) $\frac{1}{6}$ and $\frac{1}{8}$ (d) $\frac{1}{12}$ and $\frac{1}{8}$

9. If 18 children travel by car, how many children took part in the survey?

(a) 36 (b) 144
(c) 18 (d) 72

Directions (Q. Nos. 10-12) *In the following pie chart, students studying in different countries. Read it carefully and answer the following questions :*

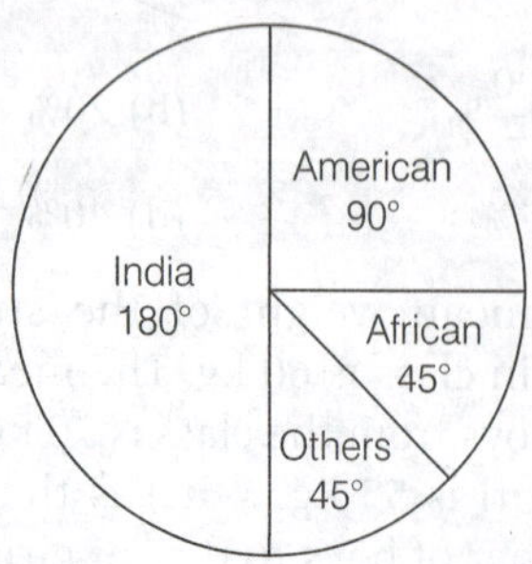

10. What is the percentage of Indian students?

(a) 25% (b) 50% (c) 75% (d) 20%

11. What is the percentage of African students?

(a) $12\frac{1}{2}\%$ (b) 25%
(c) 20% (d) 50%

12. What is the fraction of the central angle of others students?

(a) $\frac{1}{4}$ (b) $\frac{1}{12}$
(c) $\frac{1}{3}$ (d) $\frac{1}{8}$

Directions (Q. Nos. 13-15) *The following pie-chart represents the marks scored by a students, which is obtained from total marks 540, answer the following questions :*

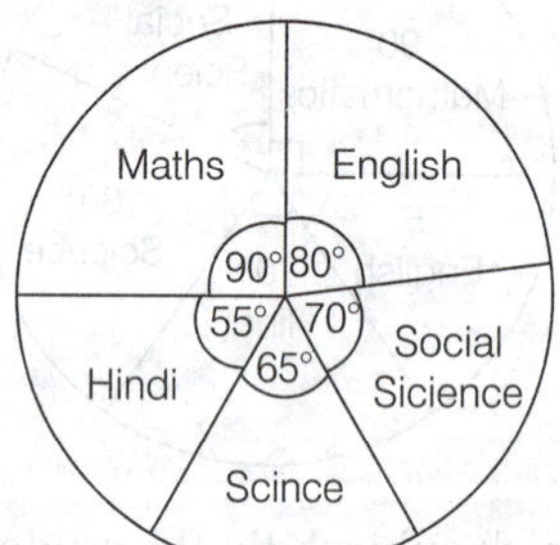

13. In which subject did the student score 120 marks?

(a) English (b) Science
(c) Maths (d) Hindi

14. What is the difference in the marks obtained in Maths and English?

(a) 15 marks (b) 20 marks
(c) 50 marks (d) 35 marks

15. In which subject did he get minimum marks?

(a) Science (b) English
(c) Maths (d) Hindi

Directions (Q. Nos. 16-18) *The histogram shows the pollution emission per week of a number of cars in a city.*

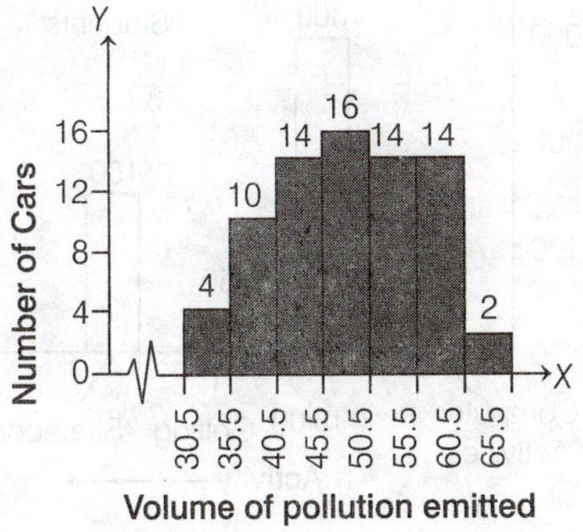

16. How many cars emits pollution below than 45.5?

(a) 28 (b) 26 (c) 44 (d) 36

17. How many cars emit pollution more than 55.5?

(a) 14 (b) 26 (c) 16 (d) 30

18. How much amount of pollution do the 10 cars emits?

(a) 40.5-45.5 (b) 30.5-35.5

(c) 60.5-65.5 (d) 35.5-40.5

Directions (Q. Nos. 19-21) The graph shows the temperature forecast and the actual temperature of a town on 8 days.

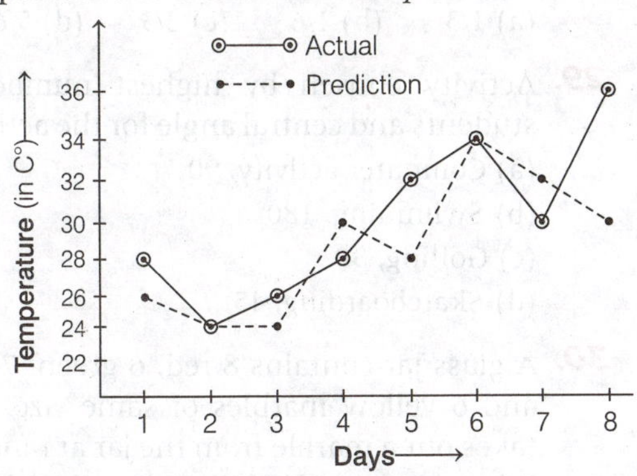

19. For how many days the actual temperature is high in comparison to prediction?

(a) 2 (b) 3

(c) 4 (d) 5

20. For how many days the prediction and actual temperature is same?

(a) 1 (b) 3

(c) 5 (d) 2

21. On which day, the graph shows the maximum deviation of actual temperature from the forecast?

(a) Day 8

(b) Day 5

(c) Day 1

(d) Day 4

22. A die is thrown, the probability of getting a multiple of 3 is

(a) $\frac{1}{2}$

(b) $\frac{1}{3}$

(c) $\frac{1}{4}$

(d) $\frac{1}{6}$

23. From a pack of well-shuffled cards, what is the probability of getting a red card of ace?

(a) $\frac{1}{26}$

(b) $\frac{3}{26}$

(c) $\frac{5}{26}$

(d) None of the above

2 Marks Questions

Directions (Q. Nos. 24-26) *The pie-chart given below represents the expenditure on different items in constructing a flat in Delhi. If the expenditure incurred on cement is ₹ 112500, then find.*

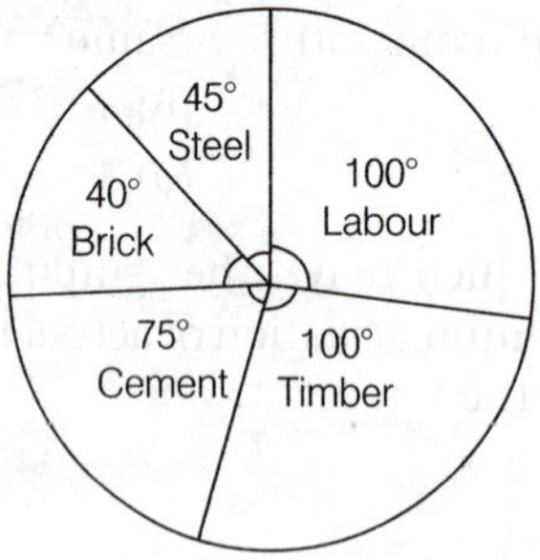

24. The total cost of the flat are

(a) ₹ 340000
(b) ₹ 5400
(c) ₹ 540000
(d) ₹ 13400

25. Expenditure incurred on labour in flat constructing are

(a) ₹ 150000
(b) ₹ 15000
(c) ₹ 125000
(d) ₹ 135000

26. The ratio between expenditure incurred on cement and the total cost of the flat is

(a) 3 : 5
(b) 5 : 21
(c) 5 : 24
(d) 5 : 34

Directions (Q. Nos. 27-29) *The bar graph given below shows the favourite summer activities of 600 students of a school. By converting the graphical representation into a pie-chart, answer the following questions carefully.*

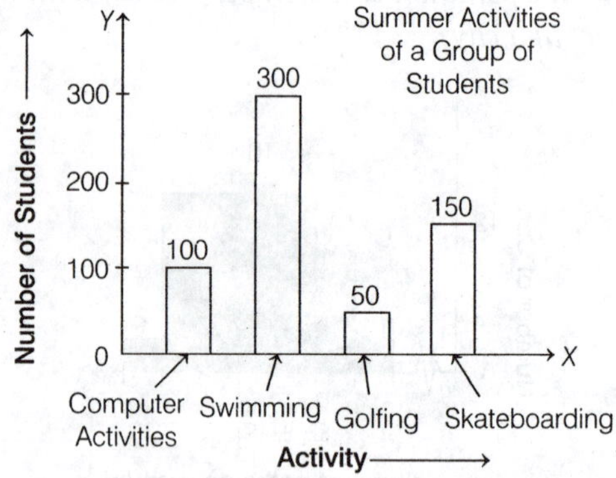

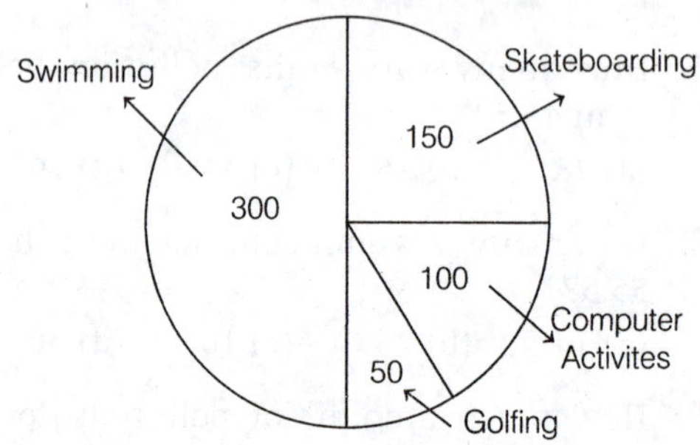

27. What is the central angle for computer activities?

(a) 90° (b) 30° (c) 60° (d) 45°

28. What is fraction of central angle for Golfing and Skateboarding together ?

(a) 1/3 (b) 1/6 (c) 2/3 (d) 5/6

29. Activity chosen by highest number of students and central angle for the activity.

(a) Computer activity, 90
(b) Swimming, 180°
(c) Golfing, 30°
(d) Skateboarding, 45°

30. A glass jar contains 8 red, 6 green, 7 blue and 6 yellow marbles of same size. Hari takes out a marble from the jar at random. What is the probability that the chosen marble is of red colour?

(a) $\frac{3}{10}$ (b) $\frac{7}{10}$ (c) $\frac{4}{5}$ (d) $\frac{2}{9}$

PRACTICE SET 01

1 Mark Question

1. Two numbers are in the ratio 4 : 5. If sum of these two numbers is 27. Then, the product of numbers is

(a) 190 (b) 180

(c) 225 (d) 240

2. Simplify $\frac{\sqrt{441}+\sqrt{196}}{\sqrt{1024}-\sqrt{324}}$.

(a) $\frac{2}{5}$ (b) $\frac{2}{3}$

(c) $\frac{5}{3}$ (d) $\frac{5}{2}$

3. The product of a rational number and its multiplicative inverse is always equal to

(a) 0 (b) −1

(c) 1 (d) its reciprocal

4. *RENT* is a rectangle. Its diagonals meet at *O*. The value of *x*, if $OR = 2x + 4$ and $OT = 3x + 1$, is

(a) 4 (b) 3

(c) 5 (d) 6

5. A shopkeeper earns a profit of 12% after selling a book at 10% discount on printed price. Then, the ratio of the cost price and printed price of the book is

(a) 45 : 56 (b) 50 : 61

(c) 99 : 125 (d) None of these

6. For how many 3-digit perfect cubes, the sum of the digits is not a perfect square?

(a) 1 (b) 2

(c) 3 (d) 4

7. The value of *m* for given expression $3^m \div 3^{-3} = 3^4$ is

(a) 6 (b) 5

(c) 1 (d) 0

8. If $x * y = x + y - \sqrt{xy}$, then the value of $7 * 63$ is equal to

(a) 63 (b) 49

(c) 21 (d) 7

9. An expression is to be written in the form of $x^2 - (a+b)x + ab$, where *a* and *b*, $(a, b > 0)$ are such that sum of their squares is 20 and difference of their squares is 12. The expression is

(a) $x^2 + 6x - 12$ (b) $x^2 - 6x + 8$

(c) $x^2 - 8x + 12$ (d) $x^2 - 8x + 16$

10. In what time will ₹1000 amount to ₹1331 at 10% per annum compounded annually?

(a) 5 yr (b) 2.5 yr

(c) 3 yr (d) 3.5 yr

11. What is the length of the diagonal of a square whose area is 19600 m^2?

(a) 140 m (b) 130 m

(c) $130\sqrt{2}$ m (d) $140\sqrt{2}$ m

12. Sum of three numbers is 105. If the ratio between first and second numbers is 2 : 3 and between second and third numbers is 4 : 5. Then, the second number is

(a) 35 (b) 24

(c) 36 (d) 45

13. Evaluate and mark the correct option.

$$[(24^2 + 7^2)^{1/2}]^3$$

(a) 625 (b) 25

(c) 1025 (d) None of these

14. One of the factors of the quotient when the polynomial $y^3 - 2y^2 - 9y + 18$ is divided by binomial $y - 2$.

(a) $(y + 3)$ (b) $(3 - y)$

(c) $(2 - y)$ (d) $(y^2 + 9)$

15. If the measure of two adjacent angles A and B of a parallelogram are in the ratio 3 : 2, then the measure of the angle opposite to angle A is

(a) 72° (b) 108°
(c) 90° (d) 144°

16. Which value of z for equation $z-\frac{z-2+2z}{4}=2z-\frac{4+3z}{2}$ is true?

(a) 4 (b) 0
(c) 10 (d) 1

17. Which of the following numbers has no reciprocal?

(a) 1 (b) −1
(c) 0 (d) 5

18. $\sqrt{41-\sqrt{29-\sqrt{18-\sqrt{4}}}}$ is equivalent to

(a) 2 (b) 4
(c) 6 (d) 5

19. The value of the given expression $\frac{7.25\times7.25\times7.25+1.75\times1.75\times1.75}{9}$ is

(a) 42.93 (b) 40.42
(c) 24.49 (d) None of these

20. How old is Rakesh?

I. Five years before, the age of Rakesh and his father was in ratio 1 : 3.

II. Five years hence, sum of their ages will be 50 yr.

(a) Only I is needed to answer the question
(b) Both I and II are needed to answer the question
(c) Only II is needed to answer the question
(d) Either I or II is sufficient

21. If $(2^{3x-1}+10)\div6=7$, then x is equal to

(a) −2 (b) 0
(c) 1 (d) 2

22. If the value of $(7+3x)$ is equal to $(7-3x)$, then the value of $(7x^2+4x+9)$ is equal to

(a) 11 (b) 9
(c) 20 (d) 3

23. Which of the property of rational number is followed by the given expression?

$$\frac{4}{5}\left\{\frac{2}{5}-\frac{4}{5}\right\}=\frac{4}{5}\times\frac{2}{5}+\frac{4}{5}\times\left(-\frac{4}{5}\right)$$

(a) Commutativity
(b) Associativity
(c) Distribution of multiplication over addition
(d) All of the above

24. If $\frac{25\times a^{-4}}{5^{-3}\times10\times a^{-8}}=x\times a^4$. Then, the value of x is

(a) 5^3 (b) 5^4
(c) $\frac{1}{2}\times5^4$ (d) 5^2

25. After solving the expression $(3^{-4}+4^{-3}+5^{-1}+6^{-2}+7^{-1})^0$, we will get

(a) 22 (b) −1
(c) 1 (d) 0

26. Simplify $\sqrt[3]{\sqrt{0.015625}}$.

(a) 0.05 (b) 0.5
(c) 5 (d) None of these

27. If ₹ 700 becomes ₹ 952 in 3 yr at a certain rate of simple interest. If the rate of interest is increased by 25%, what amount will ₹ 800 become in 3 yr?

(a) ₹ 1008 (b) ₹ 1160
(c) ₹ 1052 (d) None of these

28. If $xyz=8$ and $x+y+z=8$, then $\frac{1}{xy}+\frac{1}{yz}+\frac{1}{xz}$ is equal to

(a) 0 (b) 1
(c) 8 (d) 64

29. The sum of two numbers is 11. Five times one number is equal to 6 times the other. The bigger of the two numbers is

(a) 5 (b) 6 (c) 8 (d) 9

30. Ravi had to arrange 9604 flowers in rows such that the number of rows is equal to the number of flowers in each row, find how many rows must be formed?

(a) 78 (b) 92

(c) 98 (d) 88

31. The volume V, of a Hollow cylinder is given by formula $V = \pi(R^2 - r^2)h$. Find the value of V given that $R = 8$, $r = 5$, $h = 3\frac{1}{2}$ and $\pi = \frac{22}{7}$.

(a) 393 (b) 429

(c) 492 (d) 294

32. The value of x, if $6:8::x:15$, is

(a) 20 (b) $\frac{45}{4}$

(c) $\frac{26}{5}$ (d) None of these

33. What is the shape of the given tent?

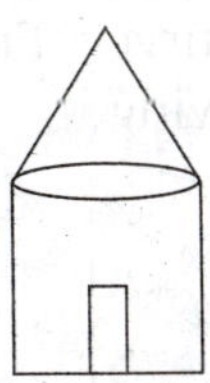

(a) A cylinder surmounted on a cone

(b) A cone surmounted on a cube

(c) A cylinder surmounted on a cube

(d) A cone is surmounted on a cylinder

34. Which of the following statements is necessarily true about division of the two rational numbers?

(a) Division of two rational numbers is closed under rational numbers.

(b) Division of two rational numbers is commutative.

(c) Both (a) and (b).

(d) None of the above

35. Simple interest on an amount for two years at the rate of 6% per annum is ₹ 300. Then, the compound interest on the same amount for the same time period and same rate of interest will be

(a) ₹ 310 (b) ₹ 308

(c) ₹ 307 (d) ₹ 309

36. As we know that, weight and length of a rod is directly proportion. If 6 m long rod can weight 30 kg and 7 m long rod can weight 35 kg. Then, how much weight a 25 m long rod can have?

(a) 105 kg (b) 250 kg

(c) 125 kg (d) 140 kg

37. Two matchsticks each of length 7 cm are crossing each other such that they bisect each other at right angles. What shape will be formed by joining their end points?

(a) Rectangle (b) Square

(c) Rhombus (d) Parallelogram

38. Which multiplication is incorrect shown below?

(i) $(a + b) \times (2a - 3b + c) = 2a^2 - ab + ac + bc - 3b^2$

(ii) $(7xy + 5y) \times 3xy = 21y^2x^2 + 15xy^2$

(iii) $(x + y)(x^2 - xy + y^2) = x^3 + y^3 + x^2y$

(iv) $2x(z - x - y) = 2xz + 2x^2 - 2xy$

Options

(a) Only (i) (b) Only (i) and (ii)

(c) Only (iii) (d) Only (iii) and (iv)

39. By what least number should 33075 be multiplied to obtain a perfect cube?

(a) 15 (b) 21 (c) 35 (d) 30

40. If $\frac{17 - 3x}{5} - \frac{4x + 2}{3} = 5 - 6x + \frac{7x + 14}{3}$, then the value of x is equal to

(a) 2 (b) 4

(c) 6 (d) 3

2 Marks Question

41. If $x = 2$ and $y = -1$, then the value of algebraic expression $\left(\frac{3}{4}x^2y\right) \times \left(\frac{-15}{4}xy^2\right) \times \left(\frac{7}{9}x^2y^2\right)$ is equal to

(a) 126 (b) 56 (c) 54 (d) 256

42. A rectangular piece of paper 44 cm $\times$ 7 cm is folded to make a cylinder of height 7 cm. Find its volume.

(a) 786 cm^3
(b) 1078 cm^3
(c) 1188 cm^3
(d) 726 cm^3

43. In the given figure, if $ABCD$ is a rhombus and $\angle BCD = 80°$, then the values of x and y respectively are

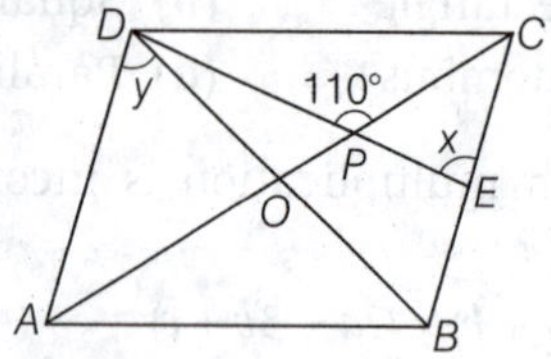

(a) 42° and 20° (b) 70° and 50°
(c) 80° and 30° (d) 50° and 40°

44. If $\frac{1}{5} : \frac{1}{x} = \frac{1}{x} : \frac{1}{125}$, then the value of x is

(a) 20 (b) 5
(c) 25 (d) 125

45. In a ticket number 1 to 40, the probability of getting a ticket number is the multiple of 4, is

(a) $\frac{7}{40}$ (b) $\frac{1}{2}$ (c) $\frac{1}{4}$ (d) $\frac{1}{5}$

46. 4% of income of P is equal to 12% of income of Q and 8% of income of Q is equal to 16% of income of R. If R's income is ₹ 2000, then the total income of P, Q and R is

(a) ₹ 6000 (b) ₹ 14000
(c) ₹ 18000 (d) ₹ 20000

47. Consider the given below figure:

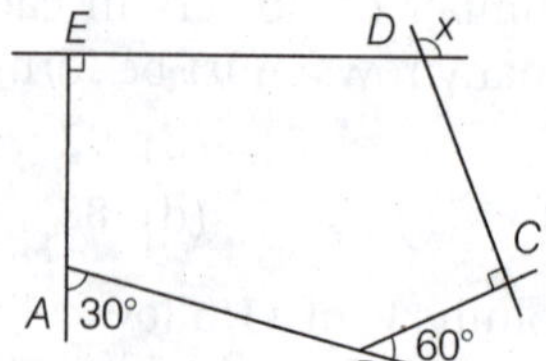

Find the value of x.

(a) 60° (b) 90° (c) 120° (d) 150°

48. The age of a man is same as his wife's age with the digits reversed. Then, sum of their ages is 99 yr and the man is 9 yr older than his wife. Man's age is

(a) 52 yr (b) 49 yr
(c) 44 yr (d) 54 yr

Directions (Q. Nos. 49 and 50) A survey was made to find the type of music that a certain group of young people liked in a city. The adjoining pie chart shows the findings of this survey. From this pie chart, answer the following

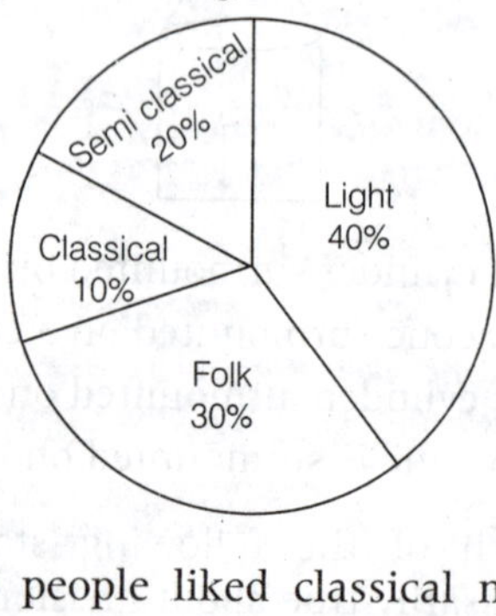

49. If 20 people liked classical music, how many young people were surveyed?

(a) 2000 (b) 150
(c) 50 (d) 200

50. If a cassette company were to make 1000 CD's, how many of semi-classic would they make?

(a) 150 (b) 50
(c) 200 (d) 100

PRACTICE SET 02

1 Mark Questions

1. $(p-2)$ is the one of factor of following expressions.

(a) p^2+6p+8 (b) $p^2-10p+21$
(c) $p^2+6p-16$ (d) None of these

2. $ABCD$ is a parallelogram, given in the figure. It is also given that, $OB=4$ and AC is 5 more than BD. The value of OA is

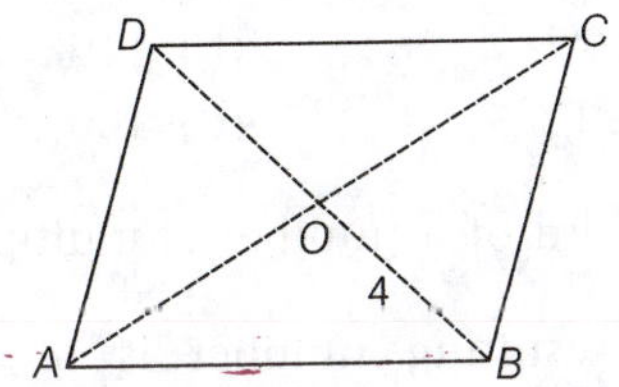

(a) 13 (b) 6.5 (c) 7 (d) 9

3. If $\frac{7y+4}{y+2}=-\frac{4}{3}$, then the value of y is equal to

(a) $-\frac{4}{5}$ (b) $\frac{2}{5}$ (c) $-\frac{2}{15}$ (d) $-\frac{3}{5}$

4. If $p * q = p - q + \sqrt{pq}$, then $18 * 8$ is equal to

(a) 20 (b) 22 (c) 24 (d) 10

5. The value of $\sqrt{\frac{(0.02)^2+(0.18)^2+(0.42)^2}{(0.002)^2+(0.018)^2+(0.042)^2}}$ is

(a) 0.1 (b) 10
(c) 10^2 (d) 10^3

6. If $\frac{2}{5}\times\left(\frac{-8}{9}\right)+P\times\frac{5}{9}=\frac{2}{5}\times[q+r]$, then p, q and r are

(a) $\frac{2}{5},\frac{8}{9},\frac{5}{9}$ (b) $\frac{2}{5},\frac{8}{9},-\frac{5}{9}$

(c) $-\frac{2}{5},-\frac{8}{9},-\frac{5}{9}$ (d) $-\frac{2}{5},-\frac{8}{9},\frac{5}{9}$

7. In a pack of card, the probability of getting a black king is

(a) 3/26 (b) 1/26
(c) 5/26 (d) 1/52

8. The profit earned by selling an article for ₹ 317 is equal to loss incurred when the same article is sold for ₹ 233. The SP of article in order to gain of 20% is

(a) ₹ 390 (b) ₹ 370
(c) ₹ 350 (d) ₹ 330

9. If the ratio between sum of exterior angles and interior angles of a regular polygon is 1:5, then the number of sides of polygon is

(a) 5 (b) 8
(c) 12 (d) 10

10. Simplify $\sqrt{\frac{(0.0144)\times(0.0289)}{(0.0025)\times(0.0441)}}$.

(a) $\frac{12}{31}$ (b) $\frac{64}{39}$

(c) 60 (d) $\frac{68}{35}$

11. Which of the following steps in calculation of compound interest is wrong?

I. $P=$ ₹ 10000, $r=10\%$, $t=1\frac{1}{2}$ yr compounded half-yearly

II. $A=P\left(1+\frac{r}{100}\right)^n$

III. $n=3$, $r=10\%$

IV. $A=$ ₹ $10000\left(1+\frac{10}{100}\right)^3$

V. CI $= A - P =$ ₹ 1576.2

(a) II (b) Both III and IV
(c) IV (d) Both IV and V

12. If $\frac{a}{b}=\frac{4}{3}$, find the value of $\frac{a^2+b^2}{a^2-b^2}$.

(a) 25/7 (b) 26/7
(c) 25/4 (d) 4

13. The value of y for given expression $\left(\frac{5}{3}\right)^{-4}\times\left(\frac{5}{3}\right)^{-5}=\left(\frac{5}{3}\right)^{3y}\times\left(\frac{5}{3}\right)^{0}$ is

(a) 3 (b) -3
(c) 0 (d) -1

14. Sanju has currency notes of denominations ₹ 100, ₹ 500 and ₹ 1000, respectively. The ratio of the number of these notes is 2 : 3 : 5. The total cash with Sanju is ₹ 20100. How many notes of ₹ 500 denomination does he have?

(a) 2 (b) 6
(c) 9 (d) 15

15. The value of the expression $\frac{2}{5}\times\frac{5}{2}-\frac{2}{5}\times\frac{5}{4}$ is

(a) 0 (b) 1
(c) $\frac{1}{2}$ (d) -1

16. The value of x in the expression $28\sqrt{x}+1426=\frac{3}{4}$ of 2872 is

(a) 576 (b) 676
(c) 1296 (d) 1444

17. Sum of the digits of a 2-digit number is 11. When we interchange the digits, it is found that the resulting new number is greater than the original number by 27. What is new number?

(a) 74 (b) 92
(c) 47 (d) 65

18. Three consecutive integers are such that when they are taken in decreasing order and multiplied by 5, 6 and 7 respectively, they add upto 214. The average of the numbers is

(a) 11 (b) 12
(c) 10 (d) 9

19. Which of the following is not factor of expression $15pq+15+9q+25p$?

(a) 1 (b) $(5p+3)$
(c) $(3p+5)$ (d) $(3q+5)$

20. Divya purchased 11 books for ₹ 10 and sold all books at the rate of 10 for ₹ 11. Then, profit/loss per cent is

(a) 10% (b) 11%
(c) 21% (d) 100%

21. If $\left(\frac{2}{3}\right)$rd of a number is multiplied by $\frac{3}{4}$, the resulting number is 6. Then, the number is

(a) 9 (b) 12
(c) 36 (d) 54

22. Manish borrowed a sum of ₹ 2000 at 20% per annum at compound interest compounded half-yearly. Immediately, he lends it another person at the same rate on the condition that the interest is compounded for every $\frac{1}{4}$th year. The amount gained by Manish in 1 yr is

(a) ₹ 11.01 (b) ₹ 12.02
(c) ₹ 13.03 (d) ₹ 14.04

23. Solution of the equation for value of x. $x-\frac{x+1}{4}=2-\frac{x-3}{3}$ is

(a) $\frac{13}{3}$ (b) 3
(c) -3 (d) 15

24. The ratio which $\left(\frac{1}{3} \text{ of ₹}9.30\right)$ is to (0.6 of ₹1.55) is

(a) 1 : 3 (b) 10 : 3
(c) 3 : 10 (d) 3 : 1

25. Which of the following is additive inverse of $\frac{250}{625}$?

(a) $\frac{625}{250}$ (b) $-\frac{625}{250}$
(c) $-\frac{2}{5}$ (d) 0

26. What number should be added to 2200 to make it a perfect square?

(a) 12 (b) 4
(c) 9 (d) 25

27. Which step is wrong in the given factorisation of a polynomial?

Step I $\rightarrow x^2 - 6x + 8$
Step II $\rightarrow x^2 - 4x - 2x + 8$
Step III $\rightarrow x(x-4) - 2(x-4)$
Step IV $\rightarrow (x-2)(x-4)$

(a) Step I
(b) Step IV
(c) Step III
(d) No Step is wrong.

28. If three angles of a quadrilateral are equal. Fourth angle is of measure 120°, then the value of equal angle is

(a) 80° (b) 90°
(c) 110° (d) 60°

29. The value of the expression $\frac{4}{25} \times \frac{2}{5} - \frac{64}{25}$ is

(a) $\frac{8}{25}$ (b) $\left(\frac{2}{5}\right)^3 \times \left(-\frac{3}{5}\right)$
(c) $\frac{2^3}{5^3}$ (d) None of these

30. If the difference between a number and its reciprocal is 5. Then, the difference between their cubes will be

(a) 140 (b) 110
(c) 125 (d) 90

31. Three persons age are in the ratio 1:2:3. If sum of youngest and eldest is 60 yr and that of middle and youngest is 45 yr. The age of eldest person will be

(a) 50 yr (b) 45 yr
(c) 40 yr (d) 30 yr

32. How long will it take a certain sum of money to triple itself at $13\frac{1}{3}$% per annum simple interest?

(a) 10 (b) 12
(c) 15 (d) 18

33. A number x is such that $5^{2x+1} \div 25 = 125$. Then, the value of x is

(a) 1 (b) 2
(c) 3 (d) 0

34. Three angles of a triangle are in the ratio 1:2:3. The sum of the smallest and greatest angles is

(a) 90° (b) 100°
(c) 120° (d) 150°

35. Multiplicative inverse of product of additive inverse of –5/2 and reciprocal of –1 is

(a) 0 (b) 1
(c) $\frac{5}{2}$ (d) $\frac{-2}{5}$

36. Ragini sold two articles. She sold one of them at 20% profit for ₹ 180 and the other at 25% loss at ₹ 150. Find her overall profit/loss percentage approximately.

(a) 5.7% loss (b) 8.8% profit
(c) 5.9% loss (d) 7.2% profit

37. If A, B, C and D are four quantities such that $A:B=3:4$, $B:C=8:9$, $C:D=15:16$. Then, $A:D$ is

(a) 5 : 8 (b) 8 : 5
(c) 4 : 5 (d) 5 : 4

38. If a rational number is such that when we multiply it by $\frac{4}{5}$ and add $\frac{2}{3}$ of it to the product, we get $-\frac{11}{5}$. Then, the number is

(a) $-\frac{1}{2}$ (b) $\frac{3}{2}$ (c) $-\frac{3}{2}$ (d) $\frac{4}{5}$

39. The multiplication of $\left(\frac{3}{4}a^2+3b^2\right)$ and $4\left(a^2-\frac{2b^2}{3}\right)$ is equal to

(a) $3a^4+10b^4-8a^2b^2$
(b) $3a^4+10a^2b^2-16b^4$
(c) $3a^4+8ab^2-10b^4$
(d) $3a^4+10a^2b^2-8b^4$

40. If $z=6$, then the value of $20z\sqrt{z^3-2z^2}$ is

(a) 1000 (b) 1040
(c) 1400 (d) 1440

2 Marks Questions

41. The value of expression

$$\frac{-\sqrt{\left(\frac{5}{3}\right)^2\times\left(\frac{3}{5}\right)^2}}{-\sqrt{\left(\frac{2}{5}\right)^3\times\left(\frac{2}{5}\right)^{-3}}}$$ is

(a) 1 (b) −1 (c) 2 (d) $\frac{25}{6}$

42. In the given figure, if $RISK$ and $CLUE$ are parallelograms. Then, the value of x is

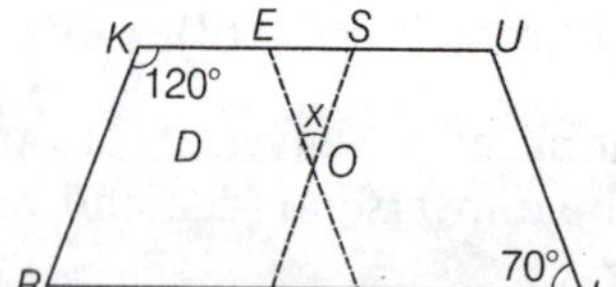

(a) 50° (b) 60°
(c) 80° (d) 70°

43. Given $\sqrt{15625}=125$, then the value of $\sqrt{156.25}+\sqrt{1.5625}$ is equal to

(a) 12.75 (b) 13.75
(c) 7.75 (d) 6.75

44. The value of $\left(\sqrt{\frac{225}{729}}-\sqrt{\frac{25}{144}}\right)\div\sqrt{\frac{16}{81}}$ is equal to

(a) $\frac{1}{48}$ (b) $\frac{15}{48}$ (c) $\frac{5}{16}$ (d) $\frac{1}{16}$

45. If $(a+b):(b+c):(c+a)=6:7:8$ and sum of the numbers a, b, c is 14. Then, the value of c is

(a) 6 (b) 8 (c) 14 (d) 7

46. Which of the following is incorrect?

(a) If $\frac{x}{2}-\frac{1}{5}=\frac{x}{3}+\frac{1}{4}$, then $x=\frac{27}{10}$

(b) If $\frac{n}{2}-\frac{3n}{4}+\frac{5n}{6}=21$, then $n=36$

(c) $x+7-\frac{8x}{3}=\frac{17}{6}-\frac{5x}{2}$, then $x=-5$

(d) $\frac{3t-2}{4}-\frac{2t+3}{3}=\frac{2}{3}-t$, then $t=1$

47. If the perimeter of the figure given is 57cm. Find the perimeter of the triangle in the figure.

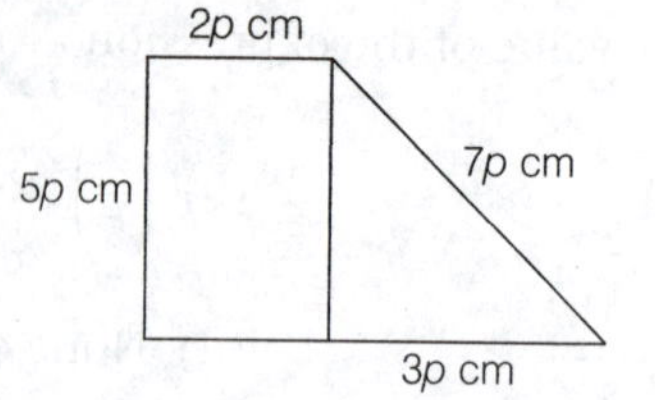

(a) 32 cm (b) 36 cm
(c) 45 cm (d) 48 cm

Directions (Q. Nos. 48-50) *The number of hours for which students of a particular class watched television during holidays is shown through the given graph. Answer the following*

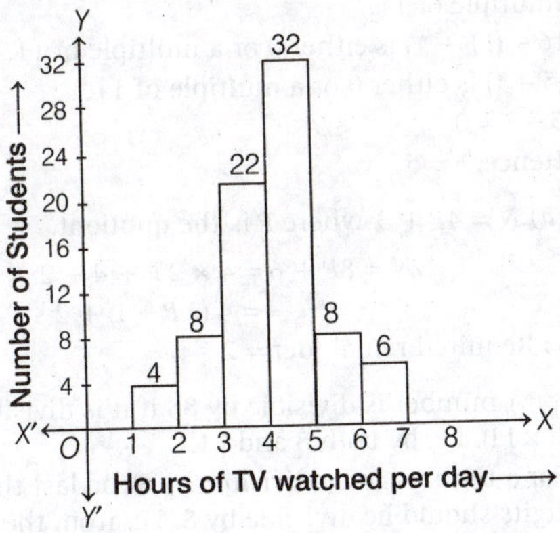

48. For how many hours did the maximum number of students watch TV?

(a) 2-3 hr
(b) 4-5 hr
(c) 3-4 hr
(d) 6-7 hr

49. How many students watched TV for less than 4 h?

(a) 34 (b) 26
(c) 28 (d) 32

50. How many students spent more than 5 h watching TV?

(a) 18 (b) 12
(c) 46 (d) 14

HINTS & SOLUTIONS

Chapter 1 : Number System

1. (a) The given number is 21 y 5.
For this number to be divisible by 9, the sum of its digits should be divisible by 9.
$\therefore$ $2+1+y+5$ is divisible by 9.
or $8+y$ is a multiple of 9.
$\therefore$ For y to be a single digit number,
$$8+y=9 \Rightarrow y=1$$

2. (d) A greatest prime number lies from 20 to 50 is 47.

3. (b) Only option (b) is satisfying the condition. 19, 13 both are prime numbers.

4. (c) Given, unit digit = 9

Then, the number must be ending with the unit digit 3 or 7. Only option (c) is satisfying the condition.

5. (d) A number is divisible by 11 if the difference between the sum of digils at even places and that of odd places is 0 or 11.

6. (b) $573xy$ is divisible by 90, (i.e., (9×10))
$\Rightarrow 573xy$ is divisible by both 9 and 10.
$\Rightarrow y=0$ as a number is divisible by 10 if its one's digit is 0.
Also, sum of digits $=5+7+3+x+0=15+x$
For divisibility by 9, $15+x=18 \Rightarrow x=3$
$\therefore$ $x+y=3+0=3$

7. (d) If the last two digits is divisible by 4, then the number $6542z8$ is divisible by 4.
So, we have $z8$ to be divisible by 4.
Therefore, greatest value of z is 8.

8. (c) N leaves remainder 0 when divided by 5.
Therefore, N is divisible by 5.
So, one's digit of N is either 0 or 5.

9. (a) If the last three digits of a number is divisible by 8, then the number is divisible by 8.
Considering option (a), 576248, last 3-digit
$$= 248 \div 8 = 31$$
So, 576248 is a multiple of 8.

10. (a) For a number to be divisible by 9, its digits sum should be divisible by 9.
$8+5+3+*+4+3+1=24+*$
3 should be written in place of * to make the sum = 27, which is divisible by 9.

11. (a) If 2735*46 is divisible by 11, then $(7+5+4)-(2+3+*+6)$ is either 0 or a multiple of 11.
$16-(11+*)$ is either 0 or a multiple of 11.
$(5-*)$ is either 0 or a multiple of 11.
$5-*=0$
Hence, * = 5.

12. (a) $N=4P+3$, where P is the quotient.
$\therefore$ $2N=8P+6=4\times 2P+4+2$
$=4(2P+1)+2$
$\Rightarrow$ Required remainder = 2

13. (c) A number is divisible by 88 if it is divisible by (8×11), i.e. by both 8 and 11.
For a number to be divisible by 8 the last three digits should be divisible by 8, i.e. from the given option, we can see that $q=6$ as 256 is divisible by 8.
$\therefore$ Sum of digits at odd places of given number
$=6+2+3=11$
Sum of digits at even place
$=5+p+9=14+p$
For divisibility by 11,
$14+p-11=0$ or multiple of 11
$3+p=11$
$\Rightarrow$ $p=8$
$\Rightarrow$ $p, q=8,6$

14. (b) Given $1^2+2^2+3^2+\ldots\ldots+512^2=m$
Now, $2^2+4^2+6^2+\ldots\ldots.+1024^2$
$=2^2(1^2+2^2+3^2+\ldots\ldots+512^2)$
$=2^2\times m$
$=4m$

15. (d) According to the question, option (d) is true.
e.g., Let $P=12$, then $Q=21$
$\therefore$ $P-Q=12-21=-9$, which is divisible by 9.

16. (c) Let the number be $xy=10x+y$
$=10x+3$ [$\because$ ones place digit = 3]
According to the question,
$$x+3=\frac{1}{7}(10x+3)$$
$\Rightarrow$ $7x+21=10x+3$
$\Rightarrow$ $-3x=-18$
$\Rightarrow$ $x=6$
$\therefore$ Required number $= xy = 63$

17. (b) It is given that, 18x71 is a multiple of 3.

$\therefore$ $1+8+x+7+1$ is a multiple of 3.

$\Rightarrow 17+x$ is a multiple of 3.

This is possible, when $17+x=0, 3, 6, 9, 12, 15, 18$ ... (i)

But x is a digit of the number 18x71.

$\therefore x$ can take values 0, 1, 2, 3,......., 9

$\Rightarrow 17+x$ can take values 17, 18, 19, 20, 21,......., 26 ... (iii)

From Eqs. (i) and (ii), we get

$$17+x=18 \text{ or } 21 \text{ or } 24$$

$$\Rightarrow \quad 17+x=18 \text{ or } x=1$$

$$\text{or} \quad 17+x=21 \text{ or } x=4$$

$$\text{or} \quad 17+x=24 \text{ or } x=7$$

$$\Rightarrow \quad x=1, 4, 7$$

18. (c) If a number is divisible by 33, then that number is also divided by 3 and 11.

Now, considering option (c), the number is 67584.

This number 67584 is divisible by 3 :

as $67584 \Rightarrow 6+7+5+8+4=30 \div 3=10$, which is divisible by 3.

Number 67584 is divisible by 11 :

$67584 \Rightarrow (8+7)-(6+5+4)=15-15=0$, so the number 67584 is divisible by 11.

19. (b) Let the required 2-digit numbers be $10a+b$ and $10p+q$ as per the condition.

We have, $a \times p=10$ and $b \times q=21$

$$a=2 \text{ and } p=5$$

$$\text{or} \quad a=5 \text{ and } p=2$$

Similarly, $b \times q=21$

$$b=3 \text{ and } q=7$$

$$\text{or} \quad b=7 \text{ and } q=3$$

Then, the possibilities are

$$10p+q=57$$

$$\Rightarrow \quad 10p+q=53 \text{ and } 10a+b=23$$

$$\Rightarrow \quad 10a+b=27$$

Since, the units digit of product 1431 is 1.

Numbers are 57 and 23 or 53 and 27.

Now, $57 \times 23=1311$ and $53 \times 27=1431$ which is given.

Hence, the required numbers are 53 and 27.

20. (a) I. True II. True III. False IV. False

Chapter 2 : Rational Number

1. (d) Zero (0) is less than every positive real number and greater then every negative rational number.

2. (c) Zero (0) has no reciprocal because it is not defined.

3. (c) $\frac{81}{27}=3$ [a natural number]

4. (c) Total number of parts in the figure = 16

Total number of shaded parts in the figure = 7

$\therefore$ Required fraction $=\frac{7}{16}$

5. (c) $\left(\frac{2}{5}+\frac{15}{25}-5\right)+\left(\frac{7}{15}\right)=\frac{2}{5}+\frac{3}{5}-5+\frac{7}{15}$

$$=\frac{5}{5}-5+\frac{7}{15}$$

$$=\frac{5-25}{5}+\frac{7}{15}=\frac{-20}{5}+\frac{7}{15}$$

$$=\frac{-60+7}{15}=-\frac{53}{15}$$

6. (b) Sum of two rational numbers = – 3

One of them $=\frac{-6}{7}$ [given]

So, other number $=-3-\left(-\frac{6}{7}\right)$

$$=\frac{6}{7}-3=\frac{6-21}{7}=-\frac{15}{7}$$

7. (c) Given, $a=\frac{1}{5}$

Then, $\left\{-\left(-\frac{a-1}{a}\right)\right\}=-\left(-1+\frac{1}{a}\right)=-(5-1)$

$$=-4=-\frac{1}{\frac{1}{4}}$$

8. (b) $4+\cfrac{1}{m+\cfrac{1}{n}}=\frac{56}{12}$ [given]

$$\Rightarrow \quad 4+\cfrac{1}{m+\cfrac{1}{n}}=4+\frac{8}{12} \qquad \left[\because \frac{56}{12}-4=\frac{8}{12}\right]$$

$$\Rightarrow \quad m+\frac{1}{n}=\frac{12}{8} \qquad \text{[by comparing]}$$

$$\Rightarrow \quad m+\frac{1}{n}=1+\frac{4}{8} \Rightarrow m+\frac{1}{n}=1+\frac{1}{2}$$

$$\Rightarrow \quad m=1, n=2 \qquad \text{[by comparing]}$$

$$\therefore \quad m+n=1+2=3$$

9. (c) According to the question,

$$\left(\frac{77}{14}+\frac{195}{26}\right)\div\left(\frac{195}{26}-\frac{77}{14}\right)$$

$$=\left(\frac{11}{2}+\frac{15}{2}\right)\div\left(\frac{15}{2}-\frac{11}{2}\right)=13\div 2=\frac{13}{2}$$

10. (c) $\frac{2}{5}\times\frac{(-3)}{7}-\frac{1}{14}-\frac{3}{7}\times\frac{3}{5}$

$=\frac{2}{5}\times\frac{-3}{7}-\frac{3}{7}\times\frac{3}{5}-\frac{1}{14}$

$=\frac{2}{5}\times\frac{(-3)}{7}+\left(\frac{-3}{7}\right)\times\frac{3}{5}-\frac{1}{14}$ (by Commutativity)

$=\frac{-3}{7}\left(\frac{2}{5}+\frac{3}{5}\right)-\frac{1}{14}$ (by distributivity)

$=\frac{-3}{7}\times 1-\frac{1}{14}=\frac{-6-1}{14}=\frac{-1}{2}$

11. (b) The distributive property of multiplication of rational numbers illustrated by the given statement.

12. (d) In the given question, Assertion is false.

e.g. Let $a=1, b=2, c=3$

Then, $a-(b-c)=(a-b)-c$

$\Rightarrow \quad 1-(2-3)=(1-2)-3$

$\Rightarrow \quad 1+1=-1-3 \Rightarrow 2\neq -4$

And reason is correct because rational numbers are not associative under subtraction.

13. (b) Let the number be x.

Then, according to the question,

$\frac{3x}{5}-\frac{2x}{7}=44$

$\Rightarrow \quad \frac{21x-10x}{35}=44 \Rightarrow 11x=44\times 35$

$\Rightarrow \quad x=4\times 35 \quad \Rightarrow \quad x=140$

$\therefore$ Sum of digits $=1+4+0=5$

14. (b) Length of cloth needed for 16 shirts = 24 m [given]

Then, length of cloth needed for 1 shirt

$=\frac{24}{16}\text{ m}=\frac{3}{2}\text{ m}$

$\therefore$ Length of cloth needed for 12 shirts

$=12\times\frac{3}{2}=18\text{ m}$

15. (c) Let total number of students be 100.

Number of students come to school by car

$=100\times\frac{2}{5}=40$

Remaining students left $=100-40=60$

Number of students come to school by bus

$=60\times\frac{1}{4}=15$

$\therefore$ Rest students $=100-(40+15)=45$

If 45 students come by walking, then total number of students = 100

If 180 students come by walking, then total number of students

$=\frac{100\times 180}{45}=400$

16. (b) Total income of Raju = ₹ 12000 [given]

Expenditure on food = ₹ $12000\times\frac{1}{4}$ = ₹ 3000

Remaining money = ₹ (12000 − 3000) = ₹ 9000

Expenditure on house rent

= ₹ $9000\times\frac{3}{10}$ = ₹ 2700

Money, saved (or left after expenditure on rent)

= ₹ (9000 − 2700) = ₹ 6300

17. (b) Improvement made by Ajay $=\frac{35}{60}-\frac{30}{60}=\frac{5}{60}$

Improvement made by Sonu

$=\frac{50}{60}-\frac{42}{70}=\frac{350-252}{420}=\frac{98}{420}=\frac{7}{30}$

We see that, $\frac{7}{30}>\frac{5}{60}$

Hence, Sonu made the most improvement.

18. (a) I. False II. True III. False IV. True V. True

19. (c) Sum of $\frac{-4}{7}$ and $\frac{5}{14}$

$=\frac{-4}{7}+\frac{5}{14}=\frac{-8+5}{14}=\frac{-3}{14}$

Sum of $\frac{9}{14}$ and $\frac{23}{14}$

$=\frac{9}{14}+\frac{23}{14}=\frac{9+23}{14}=\frac{32}{14}=\frac{16}{7}$

Now, subtracting $\frac{-3}{14}$ from $\frac{16}{7}$, we get

$\frac{16}{7}-\left(\frac{-3}{14}\right)=\frac{16}{7}+\frac{3}{14}=\frac{32+3}{14}=\frac{35}{14}=\frac{5}{2}$

20. (b) $\frac{-4}{7}+\frac{7}{6}+\frac{2}{7}+3+\left(\frac{-11}{6}\right)$

$=\left(\frac{-4}{7}+\frac{2}{7}\right)+\left(\frac{7}{6}+\left(\frac{-11}{6}\right)\right)+3$

$=\frac{-4+2}{7}+\frac{7-11}{6}+3$

$=\frac{-2}{7}+\frac{(-2)}{3}+3$

$=\frac{(-2)\times 3+(-2)\times 7}{21}+3$

$=\frac{(-6)+(-14)}{21}+3=\frac{(-20)+3\times 21}{21}$

$=\frac{-20+63}{21}=\frac{43}{21}$

21. (b) I. $-(-2) \div 2^{-1} \times 2 + 2$

$= 2 \div 1^{-1} \times 2 + 2 = 2 \div \frac{1}{2} \times 2 + 2$

$= 2 \times 2 \times 2 + 2 = 8 + 2 = 10$

II. $\left(\frac{3}{2} - \frac{2}{3}\right) - (-\square) = -\frac{1}{6}$

$\Rightarrow \quad (-\square) = \frac{3}{2} - \frac{2}{3} + \frac{1}{6}$

$\Rightarrow \quad (-\square) = \frac{9-4+1}{6}$

$\Rightarrow \quad (-\square) = \frac{6}{6} = 1$

$\therefore \quad \square = -1$

III. Given, $m * n = \frac{m}{n} - \frac{n}{m}$

$\therefore \quad 9 * 18 = \frac{9}{18} - \frac{18}{9} = \frac{1}{2} - 2 = -\frac{3}{2}$

IV. $\therefore \left(\frac{1}{4} + \frac{3}{2}\right) \div \left(\frac{1}{4} - \frac{3}{2}\right)$

$= \frac{\frac{1}{4} + \frac{3}{2}}{\frac{1}{4} - \frac{3}{2}} = \frac{\frac{1+6}{4}}{\frac{1-6}{4}} = \frac{\frac{7}{4}}{-\frac{5}{4}} = -\frac{7}{5}$

22. (b) Given, $3254p06q$ to be exactly divisible by 3 and 5, then q should be either 0 or 5 to be divisible by 5.

Now, sum of numbers $= 20 + p + q$

Now, $20 + p + q$ to be divisible by 3 should be a multiple of 3.

Considering option (b), $p + q$ should be equal to 13 such that $20 + 13 = 33$ is divisible by 3.

Hence, option (b) is correct.

23. (b) Cost of 5 hot dogs = ₹ 60

$\therefore$ Cost of 3 hot dogs $= \frac{60}{5} \times 3 =$ ₹ 36

Cost of 4 pastries = ₹ 20

$\therefore$ Cost of 2 pastries $= \frac{20}{4} \times 2 =$ ₹ 10

Cost of 3 rolls = ₹ 60

$\therefore$ Cost of 4 rolls $= \frac{60}{3} \times 4 =$ ₹ 80

$\therefore$ Total cost = ₹ (36 + 10 + 80) = ₹126

Total money Ronak have = ₹ 200

$\therefore$ Money left = ₹(200 − 126) = ₹ 74

$\therefore$ Required rational number, $\frac{p}{q} = \frac{74}{200}$

24. (a) Sugar required in first recipe

$= \frac{2}{5}$ cup of sugar

Sugar required in second recipe

= 5 tablespoons of sugar

$= 5 \times \frac{1}{15} = \frac{1}{3}$ cup of sugar

$\therefore$ More sugar needed by Ist recipe

$= \frac{2}{5} - \frac{1}{3} = \frac{6-5}{15} = \frac{1}{15}$ cup

= 1 tablespoon

25. (b) Total allowance for each of them = ₹1260

In case of Sohan,

Money left = ₹ 84

$\therefore$ The fraction of money left $= \frac{84}{1260} = \frac{1}{15}$

Since, both Mohan and Sohan are left with equal amount.

$\therefore$ Money spent at mall by Mohan

$= \left(1 - \frac{1}{15}\right) - \frac{1}{2}$

$= \frac{14}{15} - \frac{1}{2}$

$= \frac{28-15}{30} = \frac{13}{30}$

Chapter 3 : Square and Square Roots

1. (d) According to the question, $m = n^2$

Then, $\quad n = \sqrt{m}$

Hence, option (d) is correct.

2. (c) Here, $\sqrt{36} = 6$,

$\sqrt{196} = 14$ and $\sqrt{169} = 13$

But, $\quad \sqrt{181} = 13.45$

Hence, 181 is not a perfect square.

3. (d) 7 cannot be the last digit (unit's place) in a perfect square number.

4. (d) Given, $\quad x = \sqrt{169} = 13$ and $y = \sqrt{64} = 8$

$\therefore \quad x - y = 13 - 8 = 5 = E$

5. (*b*) Total number of odd numbers from 1 to 20 $= 1, 3, 5, 7, 9, 11, 13, 15, 17, 19 = 10$

$\therefore$ Sum $= (10)^2 = 100$

6. (*c*) Given, $\sqrt{4761} = 69$

Then, $\sqrt{47.61} = \sqrt{\dfrac{4761}{100}} = \dfrac{69}{10} = 6.9$

And $\sqrt{0.4761} = \sqrt{\dfrac{4761}{10000}} = \dfrac{69}{100} = 0.69$

$\therefore \sqrt{4761} + \sqrt{47.61} + \sqrt{0.4761}$
$= 69 + 6.9 + 0.69 = 76.59$

7. (*c*) $\sqrt{248 + \sqrt{52 + \sqrt{144}}}$

$= \sqrt{248 + \sqrt{52 + 12}} = \sqrt{248 + \sqrt{64}}$

$= \sqrt{248 + 8} = \sqrt{256} = 16$

8. (*d*) Given, $\sqrt{2 + \sqrt{x}} = 3$

Squaring on both sides,

$2 + \sqrt{x} = 9 \Rightarrow \sqrt{x} = 7$

$\therefore \quad x = (7)^2 = 49$

9. (*a*) Given, $\sqrt{188 + \sqrt{53 + \sqrt{y}}} = 14$

Squaring on both sides,

$188 + \sqrt{53 + \sqrt{y}} = 196$

$\Rightarrow \sqrt{53 + \sqrt{y}} = 196 - 188$

$\Rightarrow \sqrt{53 + \sqrt{y}} = 8$

Again, squaring on both sides,

$53 + \sqrt{y} = 64$

$\Rightarrow \sqrt{y} = 64 - 53 = 11$

$\therefore \quad y = (11)^2 = 121$

10. (*a*) Given, $\sqrt{1 + \dfrac{27}{169}} = \left(1 + \dfrac{x}{13}\right)$

$\Rightarrow \sqrt{\dfrac{169 + 27}{169}} = 1 + \dfrac{x}{13} \Rightarrow \sqrt{\dfrac{196}{169}} = 1 + \dfrac{x}{13}$

$\Rightarrow \dfrac{14}{13} = 1 + \dfrac{x}{13} \Rightarrow 1 + \dfrac{1}{13} = 1 + \dfrac{x}{13}$

$\therefore \quad x = 1$

11. (*a*) According to the question,

$\sqrt{\dfrac{1.69}{0.0036} \times \dfrac{1.44}{6.76}} = \sqrt{\dfrac{1.3 \times 1.3}{0.06 \times 0.06} \times \dfrac{1.2 \times 1.2}{2.6 \times 2.6}}$

$= \dfrac{1.3}{0.06} \times \dfrac{1.2}{2.6} = \dfrac{13}{6} \times 10 \times \dfrac{12}{26} = 10$

12. (*a*) In general, Pythagorean triplet is $2n, n^2 - 1, n^2 + 1$.

According to the question,

$5 = n^2 + 1 \Rightarrow n^2 = 4 \Rightarrow n = 2$

$\therefore \quad 2n = 4$

And $\quad n^2 - 1 = 4 - 1 = 3$

So, the other two numbers are 3 and 4.

13. (*b*) We know that,

Greatest five-digit number = 99999

where, $\sqrt{99999} = 316.2261$

But we have to find perfect square, so

$316 \times 316 = 99856$

14. (*b*) Total money paid

$= 1 + 3 + 5 + 7 + 9 + \ldots + 30$ terms

$= 30^2 = 900$

[since, sum of n consecutive odd numbers is n^2]

Interest paid = ₹ 150

$\therefore$ Amount borrowed = ₹ (900 – 150) = ₹ 750

15. (*c*) LCM of 6, 9, 15 $= 3 \times 2 \times 3 \times 5 = 90$

But we know that, 90 is not a perfect square.

$\sqrt{90} = 3\sqrt{10}$

For a perfect square, $3\sqrt{10} \times \sqrt{10} = 30$

$\therefore$ Square of 30 = 900

So, 900 is the smallest square number which is divisible by 6, 9 and 15.

16. (*c*) $396 = 3 \times 3 \times 2 \times 2 \times 11$

To make a perfect square, every number in its factor must be in pair.

So, the smallest number is 11.

17. (*c*) $\because \quad 80^2 = 6400$ and $\quad 85^2 = 7225$

So, 6800 lies between the squares of 80 and 85.

Also, $\quad 81^2 = 6561$

$82^2 = 6724$

$83^2 = 6889$ ... near to 6800.

Hence, 89 must be added to make the perfect square of the resultant number.

18. (*b*)

```
       72
   7 | 5190
     | 49
 142 |  290
     |  284
     |    6
```

So, 6 should be subtracted from 5190 to make it perfect square.

19. *(c)* Total amount collected = ₹ 9216

Let the number of students be x.

Then, amount contributed by each student = ₹ x

According to the question,

$\Rightarrow \quad x \times x = 9216 \Rightarrow x^2 = 9216$

$\Rightarrow \quad x = \sqrt{9216} = 96$

$\therefore$ Total number of students = 96

20. *(c)* Since, numbers are in the ratio 1 : 2 : 3.

Let the numbers be x, $2x$ and $3x$.

According to the question,

$x^2 + (2x)^2 + (3x)^2 = 224$

$\Rightarrow \quad x^2 + 4x^2 + 9x^2 = 224$

$\Rightarrow \quad 14x^2 = 224$

$\Rightarrow \quad x^2 = 16 \Rightarrow x = 4$

$\therefore$ Difference between squares of greatest and smallest numbers $= (3x)^2 - (x)^2$

$= 8x^2 = 8 \times 16 = 128$

21. *(d)* Given, $a = \sqrt{2} + 1$ and $b = \sqrt{2} - 1$

then, $a + b = 2\sqrt{2}$ and $a - b = 2$

Now, $ab = 2 - 1 = 1$ $[\because (a+b)(a-b) = a^2 - b^2]$

$$\therefore \frac{a^2 - ab + b^2}{a^2 + ab + b^2} = \frac{(a-b)^2 + ab}{(a+b)^2 - ab}$$

$$= \frac{(2)^2 + 1}{(2\sqrt{2})^2 - 1} = \frac{4+1}{8-1} = \frac{5}{7}$$

22. *(a)* I. False II. False III. False

IV. False IV. True

23. *(a)* I. Total numbers = 12

Then, sum of numbers $= (12)^2 = 144$

II. $(101)^2 - (99)^2 = (101 + 99)(101 - 99)$

$[\because a^2 - b^2 = (a+b)(a-b)]$

$= 200 \times 2 = 400$

III. $\sqrt{610 + \sqrt{212 + \sqrt{169}}} = \sqrt{610 + \sqrt{212 + 13}}$

$= \sqrt{610 + \sqrt{225}} = \sqrt{610 + 15} = \sqrt{625} = 25$

IV. The sides of a right angled triangle, whose hypotenuse is 17 cm, are 8 cm and 15 cm.

e.g. $\quad (17)^2 = (8)^2 + (15)^2$

$\Rightarrow \quad 289 = 64 + 225 \Rightarrow 289 = 289$

24. *(d)* I. Smallest perfect square is 1.

II. Sum of first 8 odd numbers $= (8)^2 = 64$

III. Given, Area of square = 144 cm^2

$\Rightarrow x^2 = 144 \Rightarrow x = 12$ cm

So, the perimeter of square $= 4 \times 12 = 48$ cm

IV. First five prime numbers = 2,3,5,7,11

Sum of square of prime numbers

$= (2)^2 + (3)^2 + (5)^2 + (7)^2 + (11)^2$

$= 4 + 9 + 25 + 49 + 121 = 208$

Now, $(14)^2 < 208 < (15)^2$.

So, 17 must be added to get perfect square.

Chapter 4 : Cube and Cube Roots

1. *(b)* $(-9)^3 = -729$ $\quad [\because \sqrt[3]{(-\text{ve})} = -\text{ve}]$

Hence, option (b) is correct.

2. *(a)* Considering option (a),

$1331 = 11 \times 11 \times 11 \Rightarrow \sqrt[3]{1331} = 11$

Hence, 1331 is a perfect cube.

3. *(b)* $\sqrt[3]{3.375} = \sqrt[3]{\frac{3375}{1000}} = \sqrt[3]{\frac{(15)^3}{(10)^3}} = \frac{15}{10} = 1.5$

4. *(c)* Considering option (c),

$$\sqrt[3]{\frac{2744}{3375}} = \sqrt[3]{\frac{14 \times 14 \times 14}{15 \times 15 \times 15}} = \frac{14}{15}$$

5. *(d)* $\sqrt[3]{(-125) \times (-3375)} = (-5) \times (-15) = 75$

6. *(b)* $\sqrt[3]{27} + \sqrt[3]{0.008} + \sqrt[3]{0.064} = 3 + 0.2 + 0.4 = 3.6$

7. *(b)* $32 = 2 \times 2 \times 2 \times 2 \times 2$

For making the perfect cube,

we multiply 32 by 2.

So, $K = 2$, i.e., $32 \times 2 = 64 = 4^3$

8. *(a)* $\sqrt[3]{288} \times \sqrt[3]{432} \times \sqrt[3]{648}$

$= \sqrt[3]{(2 \times 3 \times 4 \times 3 \times 4)(2 \times 6 \times 6 \times 6)(3 \times 6 \times 6 \times 6)}$

$= 6 \times 6 \times 3 \times 4 = 432$

9. *(c)* We have, $243 = 3 \times 3 \times 3 \times 3 \times 3$

So, to have a perfect cube root,

243 should be divided by 9.

10. *(b)* According to the question, $x^3 = 4x$

$\Rightarrow \quad x^3 - 4x = 0$

$\Rightarrow \quad x(x^2 - 4) = 0$

Either $x = 0$ or $x^2 - 4 = 0$

$\Rightarrow \quad x^2 = 4 \Rightarrow x = \pm 2$

$\because \quad x \neq 0, \; x \neq -2$

$\therefore \quad x = 2$

11. (c) Surface area of cube $= 6l^2$ [where, l is a side]

$\Rightarrow \quad 6l^2 = 150$

$\Rightarrow \quad l^2 = 25 \Rightarrow l = 5$

$\therefore$ Volume $= l^3 = (5)^3 = 125 \text{ cm}^3$

12. (c) 1A6B3

$B =$ Greatest single digit perfect cube $= 8$

and $A = 2 \times 8 - 7 = 9$

$\therefore$ Number $= 19683$

Now, $\sqrt[3]{19683} = 27$

$\therefore$ Sum $= 19683 + 27 = 19710$

13. (b) Volume of cubical tank $= 10648 \text{ m}^3$

$\therefore (\text{Side})^3 = 10648 \Rightarrow \text{Side} = \sqrt[3]{10648} = 22$

Hence, height of the tank is 22 m.

14. (a) I. True II. False III. False IV. True

15. (b) Volume of cube $= a^3 = 24389$ (Given)

$a = \sqrt[3]{24389}$

$a = 29 \text{ cm}$

$\therefore$ Total surface area $= 6a^2 = 6 \times 29 \times 29 = 5046 \text{ cm}^2$

16. (c) Given, numbers are in the ratio 2 : 3 : 4.

Let the numbers be $2x$, $3x$ and $4x$.

Then, $(2x)^3 + (3x)^3 + (4x)^3 = 33957$

$\Rightarrow \quad 8x^3 + 27x^3 + 64x^3 = 33957$

$\Rightarrow \quad x^3 = \frac{33957}{99} \Rightarrow x^3 = 343$

$\Rightarrow \quad x = \sqrt[3]{343} = 7$

$\therefore$ Difference in cubes of greatest and smallest numbers $= (4x)^3 - (2x)^3$

$= (64 - 8)x^3 = 56x^3 = 56 \times 7 \times 7 \times 7$

$= 343 \times 56 = 19208$

17. (a) **Assertion** $1729 = 1728 + 1 = (12)^3 + 1^3$

Hence, it is a Hardy-Ramanujan number.

Reason $(12)^3 = 12728$, which is true.

18. (b) I. $\sqrt[6]{\left(\frac{91125}{216}\right)^2} = \left(\frac{91125}{216}\right)^{2/6}$

$= \left(\frac{91125}{216}\right)^{1/3} = \left(\frac{45}{6}\right)^{3 \times 1/3} = \frac{45}{6}$

II. Smallest cubic number is 1.

III. $\sqrt[3]{4\frac{12}{125}} = x \Rightarrow \sqrt[3]{\frac{512}{125}} = x$

$\therefore x = \left(\frac{8}{5}\right)^{3 \times \frac{1}{3}} = \frac{8}{5}$

IV. $\sqrt[3]{729} = \sqrt[3]{27^2} = (27^2)^{1/3}$

$= (27^{1/3})^2 = (3)^2 = 9$

19. (c) Given, $\sqrt[3]{3\left(\sqrt[3]{x} - \frac{1}{\sqrt[3]{x}}\right)} = 2$

Cubing on both sides,

$3\left(\sqrt[3]{x} - \frac{1}{\sqrt[3]{x}}\right) = 8$

$\Rightarrow \quad \sqrt[3]{x} - \frac{1}{\sqrt[3]{x}} = \frac{8}{3}$ ... (i)

Cubing on both sides, we get

$x - \frac{1}{x} - 3\left(\sqrt[3]{x} - \frac{1}{\sqrt[3]{x}}\right) = \frac{512}{27}$

$\Rightarrow \quad x - \frac{1}{x} - 3 \times \frac{8}{3} = \frac{512}{27}$ [from Eq. (i)]

$\therefore \quad x - \frac{1}{x} = \frac{512}{27} + 8 = \frac{728}{27}$

Chapter 5 : Exponents and Powers

1. (b) $(x^4)^{-3} = x^{4 \times (-3)} = x^{-12}$ $[\because (x^a)^b = (x^b)^a = x^{ab}]$

2. (a) $-(-2)^3 - (-3)^2 + (-3)^4$

$= -(-8) - (9) + 81 = 8 - 9 + 81 = 80$

3. (b) $2^x + 2^x + 2^x = 192$

$\Rightarrow \quad 3 \times 2^x = 192$

$\Rightarrow \quad 2^x = 64 = 2^6$

$\therefore \quad x = 6$ [by comparing]

4. (b) $[1^{-2} + 2^{-2} + 3^{-2}] \times 6^2 = \left[1 + \frac{1}{4} + \frac{1}{9}\right] \times 36$

$= \frac{36 + 9 + 4}{36} \times 36 = 49$

5. (b) $(a^m \cdot a^n) \div \frac{a^m}{a^n} = a^{m+n} \div a^{m-n}$

$= a^{m+n-m+n} = a^{2n}$

Here, $a = 2 \Rightarrow 2^{2n}$

6. (a) Given, $(9cp^{-3})^{-2} = \frac{1}{(9cp^{-3})^2} = \frac{1}{81c^2p^{-6}} = \frac{p^6}{81c^2}$

7. (b) The standard form of 0.0000000007973

$= 79.73 \times 10^{-11}$

8. (a) $\frac{(-2)^x \times (-2)^7}{3 \times 4^6} = \frac{1}{12}$ [given]

$\Rightarrow \quad (-2)^{x+7} = \frac{3 \times 4 \times 4^5}{12}$

$\Rightarrow \quad (-2)^{x+7} = 4^5 \Rightarrow (-2)^{x+7} = (2^2)^5$

$\Rightarrow \quad (-2)^{x+7} = 2^{10} \Rightarrow (-2)^{x+7} = (-2)^{10}$

On comparing powers, we get

$x + 7 = 10 \Rightarrow x = 3$

9. (c) $\frac{5^m \times 5^3 \times 5^{-2}}{5^{-3} \times 5^{-2}} = 5^{12}$

$\Rightarrow \quad \frac{5^{m+3-2}}{5^{-3-2}} = 5^{12} \Rightarrow 5^{m+1+5} = 5^{12}$

$\Rightarrow \quad 5^{m+6} = 5^{12}$

$\Rightarrow \quad m + 6 = 12$ [by comparing]

$\therefore \quad m = 6$

10. (d) $10^m \times 10^n \times 10^p = 10^6$

$10^{m+n+p} = 10^6$

$\Rightarrow \quad m + n + p = 6$ [by comparing]

$\therefore \quad \frac{m+n+p}{3} = \frac{6}{3} = 2$

$\therefore$ Average value = 2

11. (b) $(36)^{1/2} \times 3^2 \div (27)^{1/3} = 3^x \times 2^y$

$\Rightarrow \quad 6 \times 9 \div 3 = 3^x \times 2^y$

$\Rightarrow \quad 6 \times 3 = 3^x \times 2^y$

$\Rightarrow \quad 2 \times 3 \times 3 = 3^x \times 2^y$

$\Rightarrow \quad 3^2 \times 2^1 = 3^x \times 2^y$

$\therefore \quad x = 2, y = 1$ [by comparing]

12. (c) $\frac{2^{2004} - 2^{2003}}{2^{2004} + 2^{2003}} = \frac{2^{2003}(2-1)}{2^{2003}(2+1)} = \frac{1}{3}$

13. (a) $4^x + 4^x + 4^x + 4^x = \frac{1}{512}$

$\Rightarrow \quad 4 \cdot 4^x = \frac{1}{256} \Rightarrow 4^x = \frac{1}{256 \times 4}$

$\Rightarrow \quad 4^x = \frac{1}{4^4 \times 4}$

$\Rightarrow \quad 4^x = 4^{-5} \Rightarrow x = -5$

14. (d) Given, $\frac{8^{x+1}}{2^{x-x}} = 64 \Rightarrow \frac{8^{x+1}}{2^0} = 64$

$\Rightarrow \quad 8^{x+1} = 8^2$ [$\because 2^0 = 1$]

On comparing both sides,

$x + 1 = 2$

$\Rightarrow \quad x = 1$

$\therefore \quad 3^{2x+1} = 3^3 = 27$

15. (c) $3^x \times \frac{10}{3} - 3^{x-1} = 81$

$\Rightarrow \quad 10 \times 3^{x-1} - 3^{x-1} = 81$

$\Rightarrow \quad 3^{x-1}(10-1) = 81$

$\Rightarrow \quad 9 \times 3^{x-1} = 81 \Rightarrow 3^{x-1} = 9$

$\Rightarrow \quad 3^{x-1} = 3^2$

$\Rightarrow \quad x - 1 = 2$ [by comparing]

$\therefore \quad x = 3$

16. (c) Let initial number of cells be 1.

After an hour $= 2 \times 1 = 2^1$

After 2 h $= 4 \times 1 = 2^2$

After 10 h $= 2^{10}$

$\therefore$ Number of cells $= 2^{10} = 1024$

17. (c) $512 = 2 \times 2 \times 2 \times 2 \times 2 \times 2 \times 2 \times 2 \times 2 = 2^9$

$448 = 2 \times 2 \times 2 \times 2 \times 2 \times 2 \times 7 = 2^6 \times 7^1$

$\therefore$ Sum of the powers of the prime factors

$= 9 + 6 + 1 = 16$

18. (a) $\sqrt{2\frac{1}{4} \times \left(1\frac{1}{3}\right)^2} + 1 \div \sqrt[3]{3\frac{3}{8}}$

$= \sqrt{\frac{9}{4} \times \left(\frac{4}{3}\right)^2} + 1 \div \left(\frac{27}{8}\right)^{1/3}$

$= \frac{3}{2} \times \frac{16}{9} + 1 \div \frac{3}{2} = \frac{3}{2} \times \frac{16}{9} + \frac{2}{3}$

$= \frac{8}{3} + \frac{2}{3} = \frac{10}{3} = 3\frac{1}{3}$

19. (a) Given, $\frac{2 \cdot 3^{n+1} + 7 \cdot 3^{n-1}}{3^{n+2} - 2\left(\frac{1}{3}\right)^{1-n}} = \frac{2 \cdot 3^{n+1} + 7 \cdot 3^{n-1}}{3^{n+2} - 2(3)^{n-1}}$

$= \frac{3^{n-1}(2 \times 3^2 + 7)}{3^{n-1}(3^3 - 2)} = \left(\frac{25}{25}\right) = 1$

20. (a) $2^5 \div 2^2 = 2^3 = 8$

Both (A) and (R) are true and (R) is the correct explanation of (A).

21. (c) I. True II. False III. True

IV. False,

$(4^{-1} + 8^{-1}) = \left(\frac{2}{3}\right) = (4^{-1} + 8^{-1}) \times \left(\frac{3}{2}\right)^{-1}$

$= \left(\frac{1}{4} + \frac{1}{8}\right) \times \frac{2}{3} = \frac{3}{8} \times \frac{2}{3} = \frac{1}{4}$

V. True

22. (a) Given,

$$\frac{(16)^{2m+1}\cdot 64^5}{4} = (256)^{3m+2}$$

$$\Rightarrow \quad \frac{16^{2m+1}\cdot 16^5\cdot 4^5}{4} = (256)^{3m+2}$$

$$\Rightarrow \quad 16^{2m+6}\cdot 4^4 = (16^2)^{3m+2}$$

$$\Rightarrow \quad (16)^{2m+6} = \{(16)^2\}^{3m+1} \quad [\because 4^4 = 256]$$

$$\Rightarrow \quad 2m + 6 = 6m + 2 \quad \text{[by comparing]}$$

$$\Rightarrow \quad 4m = 4; \quad \therefore \quad m = 1$$

23. (d) $(6^{30} + 6^{-30})(6^{30} - 6^{-30})$

$$= (6^{30})^2 - (6^{-30})^2$$

$$[\because (a+b)(a-b) = a^2 - b^2]$$

$$\Rightarrow \quad 6^{60} - 6^{-60} = 3^A\cdot 8^B - 3^{-A}\cdot 8^{-B}$$

$$\Rightarrow (3\cdot 2)^{60} - (3\cdot 2)^{-60} = 3^A\cdot 8^B - 3^{-A}\cdot 8^{-B}$$

$$\Rightarrow \quad 3^{60}\cdot (8)^{20} - (3^{-60})\cdot (8)^{-20} \quad [\because 2^3 = 8]$$

$$= 3^A\cdot 8^B - 3^{-A}\cdot 8^{-B}$$

On comparing, $A = 60$, $B = 20$

$\therefore \quad A + B = 80$

24. (c) $\left(\frac{81}{16}\right)^{-3/4}\times\left[\left(\frac{25}{9}\right)^{-3/2}\div\left(\frac{5}{2}\right)^{-3}\right]$

$$= \left\{\left(\frac{3}{2}\right)\right\}^{4\times\left(-\frac{3}{4}\right)}\times\left[\left(\frac{5}{3}\right)^{2\times\left(-\frac{3}{2}\right)}\div\left(\frac{5}{2}\right)^{-3}\right]$$

$$= \left(\frac{3}{2}\right)^{-3}\times\left(\frac{5}{3}\right)^{-3}\times\left(\frac{5}{2}\right)^{3}$$

$$= \left(\frac{5}{2}\right)^{3}\times\left(\frac{2}{3}\right)^{3}\times\left(\frac{3}{5}\right)^{3}$$

$$= \left(\frac{5}{2}\times\frac{2}{3}\times\frac{3}{5}\right)^{3} = (1)^3 = 1$$

25. (a) I. $(-2)^{-5} = \frac{1}{(-2)^5} = -\left(\frac{1}{2}\right)^5$

II. $4^{-2} = \frac{1}{4^2} = \frac{1}{16}$ and $(-2)^4 = (-1)^4 2^4 = +16$

$\therefore \quad 4^{-2} \neq 16$

III. $\left(\frac{8}{5}\right)^{-3}\div\left(\frac{5}{8}\right)^{2} = \left(\frac{5}{8}\right)^{3}\div\left(\frac{5}{8}\right)^{2} = \left(\frac{5}{8}\right)^{3-2} = \left(\frac{5}{8}\right)$

IV. $\left(\frac{5}{2}\right)^{-4}\times\left(\frac{5}{2}\right)^{13} = \left(\frac{5}{2}\right)^{3x} \Rightarrow \left(\frac{5}{2}\right)^{-4+13} = \left(\frac{5}{2}\right)^{3x}$

On comparing powers, we get

$-4 + 13 = 3x \;\Rightarrow\; 3x = 9 \;\Rightarrow\; x = 3$

V. $\left[\left[\left\{\left(-\frac{1}{3}\right)^2\right\}\right]^{-2}\right]^{-1} = \left[\left\{-\frac{1}{3}\right\}^{-4}\right]^{-1} = \left\{-\frac{1}{3}\right\}^{4} = \frac{1}{81}$

26. (b) I. $\left(\frac{-3}{2}\right)^3\times x = \left(\frac{4}{27}\right)^{-2}$

$$\Rightarrow x = \left(\frac{4}{27}\right)^{-2}\times\left(\frac{-2}{3}\right)^{3} = \left(\frac{27}{4}\right)^{2}\times\left(\frac{-2}{3}\right)^{3}$$

$$= \frac{27\times 27}{4\times 4}\times\frac{-2\times -2\times -2}{3\times 3\times 3} = \frac{-27}{2} = \frac{(-3)^3}{2}$$

II. $\frac{6^n}{6^{-2}} = 6^3$

$\Rightarrow \quad 6^{n+2} = 6^3 \;\Rightarrow\; n = 1$

III. $4^{n-1} = \frac{1}{4}\cdot 4^y$

$\Rightarrow \quad 4^{n-1} = 4^{y-1}$

$\Rightarrow \quad n - 1 = y - 1 \;\Rightarrow\; y = n$

IV. $-(3)^3 - (-3)^2 + (-2)^2 = -27 - 9 + 4 = -32$

Chapter 6 : Percentage

1. (b) Let the number be x.

According to the question,

$$\frac{16}{100}\times x = 72 \Rightarrow 16x = 72\times 100$$

$$\therefore \quad x = \frac{7200}{16} = 450$$

2. (a) 4 h 30 min = $(4\times 60\times 60) + (30\times 60)$

= 16200 sec

24 h = $(24\times 60\times 60)$ = 86400 sec

So, required percentage

$$= \left(\frac{16200}{86400}\times 100\right)\% = 18\frac{3}{4}\%$$

3. (c) Let ₹ x be his monthly income.

His savings = 18% of ₹ x

$$= ₹\left(x\times\frac{18}{100}\right) = ₹\,\frac{9x}{50}$$

According to the question, $\frac{9x}{50} = 3780$

$$\therefore \quad x = ₹\left(3780\times\frac{50}{9}\right) = ₹\,21000$$

4. (a) Let x be the total number of games played.

Percentage of games won = 35% of x

$$= \left(x\times\frac{35}{100}\right) = \frac{35x}{100}$$

According to the question,

$$\frac{35x}{100} = 7 \;\Rightarrow\; x = \frac{7\times 100}{35} = 20$$

5. (*b*) Let x be the number of days the school was opened.

Percentage of her attendance = 85% of x

$$= \left(x \times \frac{85}{100}\right) = \frac{85x}{100}$$

According to the question,

$$\frac{85x}{100} = 204$$

$$\therefore \quad x = \left(204 \times \frac{100}{85}\right) = 240$$

6. (*c*) Let total number of matches = x

Percentage of matches won = 60%

Then, percentage of matches lost = 40% [no match were drawn]

Given, number of match lost = 24

$\therefore$ 40% of x = 24

$$\Rightarrow \quad 40 \times \frac{x}{100} = 24 \Rightarrow x = \frac{24 \times 100}{40}$$

$$\therefore \quad x = 60$$

7. (*b*) Let one number be x.

Then, the other number = $4000 - x$

Given, 10% of $x = 6\frac{2}{3}\%$ of $(4000 - x)$

According to the question,

$$\frac{10}{100} \times x = \frac{20}{3} \times \frac{1}{100} \times (4000 - x) \quad \left[\because 6\frac{2}{3}\% = \frac{20}{3}\%\right]$$

$$\Rightarrow \quad 10x = \frac{20}{3}(4000 - x)$$

$$\Rightarrow \quad 10x = \frac{20}{3} \times 4000 - \frac{20x}{3}$$

$$\Rightarrow 10x + \frac{20x}{3} = \frac{20}{3} \times 4000$$

$$\Rightarrow \quad \frac{50x}{3} = \frac{20}{3} \times 4000 \Rightarrow x = \frac{20 \times 4000}{50} = 1600$$

The two numbers are 1600 and 2400.

$\therefore$ Their difference = 2400 − 1600 = 800

8. (*d*) Let the maximum marks be M.

According to the question,

Pass marks = 20% of M + 30 = 32% of M − 42

$$\Rightarrow \quad \frac{M \times 20}{100} + 30 = \frac{M \times 32}{100} - 42$$

$$\Rightarrow \quad M \times \left(\frac{12}{100}\right) = 72$$

$$\Rightarrow \quad M = 600$$

$\therefore$ Pass marks = 20% of 600 + 30 = 150

$$\Rightarrow \text{Percentage of pass marks} = \frac{150}{600} \times 100\% = 25\%$$

9. (*c*) Let ₹ x be the value of the machine last year.

Then, present value = 80% of ₹ x

$$= ₹\left(x \times \frac{80}{100}\right) = ₹\frac{4x}{5}$$

According to the question,

$$\frac{4x}{5} = 240000$$

$$\therefore \quad x = \left(240000 \times \frac{5}{4}\right)$$

$$\Rightarrow \quad x = 60000 \times 5 = ₹\,300000$$

10. (*c*) Given, amount of kerosene oil in beaker = 475 L

Percentage loss by leakage and evaporation = 8%

$\therefore$ Percentage after loss in the beaker = 92%

$\therefore$ Final amount = 475 L × 92%

$$= \frac{475 \times 92}{100} = 437\text{ L}$$

11. (*b*) We have, $6\frac{2}{3}\% = \frac{20}{3}\%$

$$= \left(\frac{20}{3} \times \frac{1}{100}\right) = \frac{1}{15} = 0.06$$

Also, $\frac{3}{20} = 0.15$

The 3rd number is 0.14.

Clearly, 0.15 is the largest.

Hence, $\frac{3}{20}$ is the largest.

12. (*b*) Amount of carbohydrate = 63% of 2600

$$= \left(2600 \times \frac{63}{100}\right) = 1638 \text{ calories}$$

13. (*d*) Mass of the alloy = 1 kg

Percentage of copper = 40%

Percentage of nickel = 32%

Percentage of zinc = {100 − (40 + 32)}% = 28%

$\therefore$ Mass of zinc in 1 kg of alloy $= \left(\frac{28}{100} \times 1\right)$ kg

= 0.28 kg = 0.28 × 1000 g = 280 g

14. (*a*) Let the total number of coins = x

₹ 5 coins = 20% of total

$$\Rightarrow \quad 80 = \frac{20}{100} \times x \Rightarrow x = 400$$

$\therefore$ Total number of coins = 400

15. (*d*) Let B's income be ₹ 100.

Then, A's income = ₹ 80

Therefore, B's income is more than A's income by

$$= \frac{100 - 80}{80} \times 100\% = \frac{20}{80} \times 100\% = 25\%$$

16. (d) 22-carat gold contains 22 parts pure gold out of 24 parts.

Also, 24-carat gold is given to be 100 % pure.

$\therefore$ Percentage of pure gold in 22-carat gold

$$= \left(\frac{22}{24} \times 100\right)\% = 91\frac{2}{3}\%$$

Hence, 22-carat gold contains $91\frac{2}{3}\%$ of pure gold.

17. (d) Let x be the amount of gunpowder.

Amount of nitre = 75%

Let x kg be the amount of gunpowder containing 9 kg of nitre.

i.e., (75% of x) = 9 kg

$$\Rightarrow \left(x \times \frac{75}{100}\right) = 9 \Rightarrow \frac{75x}{100} = 9$$

$$\Rightarrow x = \left(9 \times \frac{100}{75}\right) \Rightarrow x = 12\text{ kg}$$

Hence, 12 kg of gunpowder contains 9 kg of nitre.

Now, amount of sulphur = 10%

Let x kg be the amount of gunpowder containing 2.5 kg of sulphur.

i.e., (10% of x) = 2.5 kg

$$\Rightarrow \left(x \times \frac{10}{100}\right) = 2.5 \Rightarrow \frac{10x}{100} = 2.5$$

$$\Rightarrow \frac{x}{10} = 2.5$$

$$\Rightarrow x = (2.5 \times 10)$$

$$\Rightarrow x = 25\text{ kg}$$

Hence, 25 kg of gunpowder contains 2.5 kg of sulphur.

18. (a) Let ₹ x be the amount of money recieved by C.

Then, amount of money B gets = (50% of ₹ x)

Amount of money A gets = (50% of B)

= (25% of ₹ x)

Now, x + (50% of ₹ x) + (25% of ₹ x) = ₹ 7000

$$\Rightarrow x + \left(x \times \frac{50}{100}\right) + \left(x \times \frac{25}{100}\right) = ₹\ 7000$$

$$\Rightarrow x + \frac{50x}{100} + \frac{25x}{100} = ₹\ 7000$$

$$\Rightarrow \frac{175x}{100} = ₹\ 7000 \Rightarrow x = ₹\left(7000 \times \frac{100}{175}\right)$$

$$\Rightarrow x = ₹\ 4000$$

$\therefore$ C gets ₹ 4000.

Amount of money B gets = (50% of ₹ x)

= (50% of ₹ 4000)

$$= ₹\left(4000 \times \frac{50}{100}\right) = ₹\ 2000$$

19. (d) I. $7\frac{1}{2}\%$ of ₹ 1200 $= \left(\frac{15}{2}\%\text{ of } ₹1200\right)$

$$= ₹\left(\frac{15}{2} \times \frac{1}{100} \times 1200\right) = ₹\ 90$$

II. Required percentage

$$= \left(\frac{240}{3 \times 1000} \times 100\right)\% = 8\%$$

III. (x% of 35) = 42

$$\Rightarrow \left(35 \times \frac{x}{100}\right) = 42 \Rightarrow \frac{35x}{100} = 42$$

$$\Rightarrow x = \left(42 \times \frac{100}{35}\right) \Rightarrow x = 120\%$$

IV. Let the required number be x.

Then, we have : 120 = x% of 80

$$\Rightarrow \left(80 \times \frac{x}{100}\right) = 120 \Rightarrow \frac{80x}{100} = 120$$

$$\Rightarrow x = \left(120 \times \frac{100}{80}\right) \Rightarrow x = 150\%$$

Chapter 7 : Ratio and Proportion

1. (b) Direct proportion,

$$x \propto y$$

$$\Rightarrow x = Ky \qquad [K \text{ is a constant}]$$

$$\therefore \frac{x}{y} = K$$

2. (b) Given, $x = 10$, $y = 25$

$$\Rightarrow \frac{y}{x} = \frac{25}{10} = \frac{5}{2}$$

So, the possible value of x and y are 2 and 5.

3. (a) We know that

1 kg = 1000 g

$\therefore$ 2 kg = (2×1000) g = 2000 g

So, ratio of 50g and 2000g $= \frac{50}{2000} = \frac{1}{40} = 1:40$

4. (b) Given, $A : B = 3 : 4 = a : b$

and $B : C = 6 : 5 = c : d$

So, $A : B : C = ac : bc : bd = 3 \times 6 : 4 \times 6 : 4 \times 5$

$= 3 \times 3 : 4 \times 3 : 2 \times 5 = 9 : 12 : 10$

5. (c) Let the angles be $4x$, $5x$, $9x$.

We know,

Sum of angles in a triangle = 180°

$$4x + 5x + 9x = 180° \Rightarrow 18x = 180°$$

$$\Rightarrow x = \frac{180°}{18} = 10°$$

$\therefore$ Angles are $4 \times 10° = 40°$, $5 \times 10° = 50°$ and $9 \times 10° = 90°$

6. *(c)* Consumed diesel = 54 L

Distance covered = 297 km

$\therefore$ Distance/litre $= \frac{297}{54}$ km $= \frac{11}{2}$ km

Now, distance = 550 km

$\therefore$ Consumed diesel $= 550 \div \frac{11}{2} = 100$ L

$\therefore$ Required diesel = 100 L − 54 L = 46 L

7. *(a)* According to the question,

$$x_1 = 6, y_1 = 4$$

$$\Rightarrow \frac{x_1}{y_1} = \frac{6}{4} = \frac{3}{2} \text{ and } x_2 = 12, y_2 = 8$$

$$\Rightarrow \frac{x_2}{y_2} = \frac{12}{8} = \frac{3}{2}$$

i.e., $\frac{x_3}{y_3} = \frac{3}{2} = K\ldots$ [fixed]

So, $\frac{x_1}{y_1} = \frac{x_2}{y_2} = \ldots = K$

i.e., increase in $x \propto$ increase in y

Hence, $x \propto y$

8. *(c)* Total men = 100

Food available for 24 days.

Added persons = 20

$\therefore$ Total available persons = 100 + 20 = 120

So, number of days, they will enjoy the food

$$= \frac{24 \times 100}{120} = 20$$

9. *(b)* Total time of schooling $= 30 \times 8$

$= 240$ min

Now, total number of periods = 10

$\therefore$ Duration of each period $= \frac{240}{10}$ min = 24 min

10. *(b)* Number of men working originally = 300

Number of working hours = 60 per week

New number of working hours = 40 per week

Let number of men working after change in working hours be x.

Since, they are inversely proportional.

Then, $300 \times 60 = 40 \times x \Rightarrow \frac{300 \times 60}{40} = x$

$\therefore$ $x = 450$

11. *(a)* Typing speed of Aman = 30 words per minute

Time taken to finish the essay = 2 h = 2×60 min

Let Kali speed be x words per minute.

And time required to type the essay = 1.5 h

$= 1.5 \times 60$ min

Since, they are inversely proportional.

$\therefore$ $30 \times 2 = 1.5x$

$$\Rightarrow x = \frac{30 \times 2 \times 60}{1.5 \times 60} = 40 \text{ words per minute}$$

12. *(c)* Number of fans = 50

Cost of fans = ₹ (50 × 500) = ₹ 25000

New cost of each fan = ₹(500 + 20) = ₹520

$\therefore$ Number of fans in that amount $= \frac{25000}{520} \approx 48$

13. *(b)* 8 persons complete a piece of work = 6 days

1 person complete a piece of work = (6×8) days

$\therefore$ 6 persons complete a piece of work

$$= \frac{6 \times 8}{6} \text{ days} = 8 \text{ days}$$

14. *(b)* In 1 day, the number of cows graze the field

$= 60 \times 15$

So, in 10 days, the number of cows graze the field $= \frac{60}{10} \times 15 = 90$

15. *(b)* Average speed while going to school

= 12 km/h

Time taken to reach school = 20 min $= \frac{20}{60}$ h

$\therefore$ Speed needed to reach school in 15 min $\left(\text{or } \frac{15}{60}\right)$ h

$$= \frac{12 \times 20/60}{15/60} = 16 \text{ km/h}$$

16. *(b)* Given, 30 km distance covered in 30 min.

$\therefore$ 15 km distance covered $= \frac{30}{30} \times 15 = 15$ min

$$= \frac{15}{60} \text{ h} = \frac{1}{4} \text{ h}$$

17. *(c)* $\frac{5}{8}$ work is done in 10 days.

1 work is to be done in $10 \times \frac{8}{5} = 16$ days.

$\therefore$ $\frac{3}{4}$ work $= \frac{16 \times 3}{4} = 12$ days

$\therefore$ Number of extra days = 12 − 10 = 2

18. *(a)* I. False II. True III. True IV. True

19. *(d)* Quantity of petrol = 33 L

Distance covered = 363 km

Consumption per km = $\frac{363}{33} = 11$ km/L

New Distance = 407 km

New Quantity = $\frac{407}{11} = 37$ L

Rate = ₹ 78 /L

$\therefore$ Total cost = $37 \times 78 =$ ₹ 2886

20. (b) Five years ago, the ratio of son's and his mother's age = 2 : 5

Let age of son = $2x$ yr

and age of mother = $5x$ yr

After 5 yr, age of son = $(2x + 5) + 5 = (2x + 10)$ yr

Age of mother = $(5x + 5) + 5 = (5x + 10)$ yr

According to the question,

$$\frac{2x+10}{5x+10} = \frac{4}{7}$$

$\Rightarrow \quad 14x + 70 = 20x + 40$

$\Rightarrow 6x = 30 \Rightarrow x = 5$

$\therefore$ Present age of son = $2x + 5 = 2 \times 5 + 5 = 15$ yr

21. (b) Cost of 2 watches = Cost of 3 fans

= ₹1500

2 watches = 3 fans

$\Rightarrow \quad 1 \text{ watch} = \frac{3}{2}$ fans

$\Rightarrow 6 \text{ watches} = \frac{6 \times 3}{2}$ fans = 9 fans

$\therefore$ Total number of fans (6 fans + 6 watches)

= (6 + 9) fans = 15 fans

$\therefore \quad$ Total cost = $\frac{1500}{3} \times 15 =$ ₹ 7500

22. (b) I. directly proportional

II. decreases

III. $A : B = 2 : 3 = 2 \times 4 : 3 \times 4 = 8 : 12$

$B : C = 4 : 5 = 4 \times 3 : 5 \times 3 = 12 : 15$

$\therefore A : C = 8 : 15$

IV. 12:1

23. (a)

I. $\frac{2}{5}$th of work is completed in 10 days.

Full work is completed in $\frac{10 \times 5}{2}$ i.e. 25 days

Half work is completed in $\frac{25}{2}$ i.e. $12\frac{1}{2}$ days

II. 30 dozens of eggs = ₹ 600

1 dozen of eggs = ₹ $\frac{600}{30}$

$\therefore$ 5 dozens of eggs = ₹ $\frac{600}{30} \times 5 =$ ₹ 100

III. Given, 5 men = 10 women

$\therefore$ 1 men = 2 women

IV. In 75 steps, divya travels = 50 m

In 1 step, divya travels = $\frac{50}{75}$ m

In 375 steps, divya travels = $\frac{50}{75} \times 375$

= 250 steps

Chapter 8 : Profit, Loss and Discount

1. (a) Profit/loss is always calculated on CP.

2. (b) Given selling price (SP) = $\frac{5}{4}$ of cost price (CP)

Let $\quad$ CP = x

Then, $\quad$ SP = $\frac{5}{4} \cdot x$

$\therefore$ Profit = SP – CP

$20 = \frac{5x}{4} - x$

$\Rightarrow \quad \frac{x}{4} = 20 \Rightarrow x = 80$

$\Rightarrow \quad$ CP = ₹ 80

SP = $\frac{5}{4} \times 80 =$ ₹ 100

$\therefore$ CP : SP = 80 : 100 = 4 : 5

3. (b) SP of 6 articles = ₹ 1; Loss = 20%

$\therefore$ CP of 6 articles

$$= \frac{1 \times 100}{(100 - 20)} = \frac{100}{80} = \frac{5}{4} = 1.25$$

If the gain is 20%, then SP of 6 articles

$$= \frac{1.25 \times 120}{100} \text{ ₹} = 1.50$$

$\therefore$ For ₹ 1,4 articles are sold.

4. (c) Let the CP for Rohan be ₹ x.

$\therefore$ Gain = 20%

$\therefore$ SP of watch for Rohan

$$= \frac{120}{100} \times ₹x = ₹\frac{120x}{100}$$

CP of watch for Mohan = ₹ $\frac{120x}{100}$

Loss = 10%

$\therefore$ SP of watch for Mohan = $\frac{90}{100} \times \frac{120x}{100} =$ ₹ $\frac{27x}{25}$

$\Rightarrow$ CP for Sohan $= \frac{27x}{25}$

Given, $\frac{27x}{25} = 216$

$\Rightarrow \quad x = \frac{25 \times 216}{27}$

$x = 25 \times 8 = ₹\ 200$

5. (c) Correct formula is given below.

$$CP = \frac{100}{(100 - Loss\%)} \times SP$$

6. (c) CP of bananas = ₹ 250,

Gain required = 20%

$\therefore$ SP of bananas $= \frac{250 \times 120}{100} = ₹\ 300$

Number of good bananas $= (40 \times 12 - 30) = 450$

$\therefore$ SP of 450 bananas $= ₹\ 300$

$\Rightarrow$ SP of 12 bananas $= ₹\ \frac{300}{450} \times 12 = ₹8$

$\therefore$ The remaining bananas should be sold at ₹8 per dozen to make a profit of 20%.

7. (b) Let cost price of bicycle for A be ₹ 100.

$\therefore$ SP of bicycle for A = CP of bicycle for B

$= ₹100 + \left(₹100 \times \frac{30}{100}\right) = ₹130$

$\therefore$ SP of bicycle for B = CP of bicycle for C

$= ₹130 - \left(₹130 \times \frac{20}{100}\right) = ₹\ 104$

If C pays ₹ 104, then CP of bicycle for A is ₹ 100.

$\because$ C pays ₹ 520, then CP of bicycle for A

$= ₹\ \frac{100 \times 520}{104} = ₹\ 500$

8. (c) CP of 5 oranges = ₹ 6

Profit per cent = 20%

$\therefore$ SP of 5 oranges $= 6 + 6 \times \frac{20}{100} = 6 + 1.2 = ₹\ 7.2$

$\therefore$ SP of 1 orange $= ₹\frac{7.2}{5} = ₹\ 1.44$

9. (c) Use formula for successive discount for $x\%$, $y\%$ and $z\%$.

First, successive discount for $x\%$, $y\%$, is

$$x + y - \frac{x \times y}{100} = r\ \% \quad \text{[say]}$$

Then, successive discount for $r\%$ and $z\%$ is $\left(r + z - \frac{r \times z}{100}\right)\%$

Now, $r\% = 20 + 10 - \frac{20 \times 10}{100} = 28\%$

$\therefore$ Final discount $= 28 + 10 - \frac{28 \times 10}{100} = 38 - 2.8$

$= 35.2\%$

Alternate Method

Final discount

$= 100 - \frac{(100 - 20) \times (100 - 10) \times (100 - 10)}{10000}$

$= 100 - \frac{80 \times 90 \times 90}{10000} = 100 - \frac{648}{10}$

$= \frac{1000 - 648}{10} = 35.2\%$

10. (a) SP of 90 ball pens = ₹160, loss = 20%

$\therefore$ CP of 90 ball pens $= ₹\ \frac{160 \times 100}{(100 - 20)}$

$= ₹\ \frac{160 \times 100}{80} = ₹\ 200$

$\therefore$ CP of 1 ball pen $= ₹\ \frac{200}{90} = \frac{20}{9}$

Suppose x ball pens are sold to earn a profit of 20%.

Then, CP of x ball pens $= ₹\ \frac{20}{9}x$

SP of x ball pens $= ₹\ 96$

$\therefore$ Profit $= ₹\left(96 - \frac{20}{9}x\right)$

Given profit % = 20%

$\therefore \quad \frac{\left(96 - \frac{20}{9}x\right)}{\frac{20}{9}(x)} \times 100 = 20$

$\Rightarrow \left(96 - \frac{20x}{9}\right) \times 5 = \frac{20x}{9}$

$\Rightarrow \quad 96 - \frac{20x}{9} = \frac{4x}{9}$

$\Rightarrow \quad x = \frac{96 \times 9}{24} = 36$

11. (c) Marked price of an article = ₹ 500

Discount percent = 5%

$\therefore$ SP of article = (MP – Discount%)

$= ₹\left(500 - 500 \times \frac{5}{100}\right) = ₹\ 475$

Profit percent = 25%

$\therefore$ CP of article $= \frac{475 \times 100}{100 + 25} = \frac{475 \times 100}{125} = ₹\ 380$

12. (a) Stores A and B charge for video game = ₹ 750

For store B, SP of video game = ₹ 600

For store A,

SP of video game $= ₹\ 750 - \left(₹\ 750 \times \frac{25}{100}\right)$

$= ₹\ 750 - (187.5) = ₹\ 562.5$

So, store *A* provides video game at less price.

13. (*c*) In option (c) only there is loss and in all other cases, there is profit.

14. (*a*) I. False II. False

III. True,

$$CP = \frac{SP \times 100}{100 + \text{Profit\%}} = \frac{810 \times 100}{100 + 8} = \frac{81000}{108} = ₹\ 750$$

IV. True V. False

15. (*c*) Given, price = ₹ 1500

Marked price (MRP) $= 1500 + 20\%$ of 1500

$= 1500 + 300 = ₹ 1800$

$\therefore$ Discount = 15% of 1800 $= \frac{15 \times 1800}{100} = 270$

$\therefore$ Amount customer has to pay $= 1800 - 270$

$= ₹\ 1530$

16. (*b*) Let CP of radio be ₹ 100.

SP of radio $= ₹(100 - 100 \times 2.5\%) = ₹\ 97.5$

Given, profit = 7.5%

$$SP = 100 + 100 \times 7.5\% = 100 + 100 \times \frac{7.5}{100} = ₹107.5$$

$\therefore$ Difference in SP $= 107.5 - 97.5 = ₹\ 10$

When difference is ₹ 10, CP of radio ₹ 100.

When difference is ₹ 100,

$$\text{CP of radio} = ₹\ \frac{100 \times 100}{10} = ₹\ 1000$$

Profit per cent = 12.5%

$$\therefore \quad SP = 1000 + 1000 \times \frac{125}{1000} = ₹\ 1125$$

17. (*b*) Let the market price be ₹ 100.

SP for the first discount series

$$= \frac{80}{100} \times \frac{85}{100} \times \frac{90}{100} \times 100 = ₹\ 61.20$$

SP for the second discount series

$$= \frac{75}{100} \times \frac{88}{100} \times \frac{92}{100} \times 100 = ₹\ 60.72$$

$\therefore$ The second discount series is more favourable.

18. (*b*) Let marked price of a pen be ₹ 100.

Discount = 20%

$$\therefore \quad SP = ₹\left(100 - 100 \times \frac{20}{100}\right) = ₹\ 80$$

$$\text{New marked price} = 100 + 100 \times \frac{20}{100} = ₹\ 120$$

Discount allowed = 20%

$$\therefore \text{ New SP} = ₹\left(120 - 120 \times \frac{20}{100}\right) = ₹\ 96$$

Now, change in SP $= ₹(96 - 80) = ₹16$

$$\therefore \text{ Percent change in SP} = \frac{16}{80} \times 100 = 20\%$$

19. (*b*) I. Given, CP = ₹ 150

loss% = 20%

$$\therefore \quad SP = \frac{100 - \text{loss\%}}{100} \times CP$$

$$= \frac{100 - 20}{100} \times ₹\ 150 = \frac{80}{100} \times 150$$

SP = ₹ 120

II. Given, SP = ₹ 250; Profit percent = 25%

$$\therefore \quad CP = \frac{100}{100 + \text{Profit\%}} \times SP$$

$$= \frac{100}{100 + 25} \times ₹\ 250 = \frac{100}{125} \times 250$$

CP = ₹ 200

III. Let the amount be ₹ 100

Profit = 10%

$$\text{Increased Amount} = \frac{100 + \text{Profit\%}}{100} \times ₹\ 100$$

$$= \frac{100 + 10}{100} \times ₹\ 100 = \frac{110}{100} \times 100 = ₹\ 110$$

Loss% = 10%

Amount after decreasing

$$= \frac{100 - \text{loss\%}}{100} \times \text{Increased Amount}$$

$$= \frac{100 - 10}{100} \times 110 = \frac{90}{100} \times 110 = ₹\ 99$$

Net Decrease = ₹ 100 − ₹ 99 = ₹ 1

$$\text{Net Loss} = \frac{₹1}{₹\ 100} \times 100 = 1\%$$

IV. Profit is only calculated when SP is greater than CP.

20. (*a*) I. Sales tax

II. $\because$ SP of 4 oranges = CP of 36 oranges − SP of 36 oranges,

SP of 40 oranges = CP of 36 oranges

Let CP of 1 orange be ₹ 1.

$\therefore$ CP of 36 oranges $= 1 \times 36 = ₹\ 36$

SP of 40 oranges = ₹ 36

$$\text{SP of 1 orange} = ₹\ \frac{36}{40} = ₹\ 0.9$$

$\because$ CP > SP

Loss = ₹ 1 − ₹ 20.9 = ₹ 0.1

$$\text{Loss\%} = \frac{\text{Loss}}{CP} \times 100 = \frac{₹\ 0.1}{₹1} \times 100 = 10\% \text{ Loss}$$

III. Let MRP be ₹ x

Given, SP = ₹ 880; Discount = 12%

$$SP = \frac{100 - Discount\%}{100} \times ₹\, x$$

$$₹\, 880 = \frac{88}{100} \times ₹\, x$$

$$x = \frac{₹\, 880 \times 100}{88} \Rightarrow x = ₹\, 1000$$

MRP = ₹ 1000

IV. MRP = ₹ 200

Sales Tax = 5%

$$\text{New MRP} = \frac{100+5}{100} \times ₹\, 200$$

$$= \frac{105}{100} \times ₹\, 200 = ₹\, 210$$

Discount % = 5%

$$\therefore SP = \frac{100-5}{100} \times ₹\, 210 = \frac{95}{100} \times 210 = ₹\, 199.5$$

Chapter 9 : Simple and Compound Interest

1. *(b)* Given, $P = 20000$; $T = 73$ days; $R = 10\%$

$$SI = \frac{P \times R \times T}{100}$$

$$\therefore \text{Time should be in years} = \frac{20000 \times 10 \times 73}{100 \times 365}$$

[1 yr – 365 days]

$$\therefore \quad SI = ₹\, 400$$

2. *(c)* Given, $P = ₹\, 12000$

Amount = ₹ 18000, $T = ?$

$R = 5\%$

$$SI = \text{Amount} - \text{Principal} = \frac{P \times R \times T}{100}$$

$$18000 - 12000 = \frac{12000 \times 5 \times T}{100}$$

$$\Rightarrow \quad 6000 = 120 \times 5 \times T$$

$$\Rightarrow \quad T = 10 \text{ yr}$$

3. *(a)* Given, $R = 8\%$, $T = ?$

SI = 0.5 principal

$$SI = \frac{1}{2}P$$

$$\text{We know,} \quad SI = \frac{P \times R \times T}{100} \Rightarrow \frac{1}{2}P = \frac{P \times 8 \times T}{100}$$

$$T = \frac{50}{8} = 6 \text{ yr and 3 months.}$$

4. *(a)* Given, $(SI) = \frac{1}{4} \times \text{Principal}$,

Rate = Time, $R = T$

$$\because \quad SI = \frac{P \times R \times T}{100}$$

$$\Rightarrow \quad \frac{1}{4}P = \frac{P \times R \times R}{100}$$

$$\Rightarrow \quad \frac{100}{4} = R^2 \Rightarrow R = 5\%$$

5. *(a)* Rate for 2 yr = 6%

Rate for next 3 yr = 9%

Total amount paid = ₹ 11400

Time = 9 yr

$P = ?$

$$SI = \frac{P \times R \times T}{100} \quad \therefore \quad \frac{P \times 6 \times 2}{100} + \frac{P \times 9 \times 3}{100} = 11400$$

$$\Rightarrow \quad 12P + 27P = 11400 \times 100$$

$$\Rightarrow \quad 39P = 11400 \times 100$$

$$\Rightarrow \quad P = \frac{11400 \times 100}{39}$$

$$\therefore \quad P = ₹\, 29230.8$$

6. *(b)* Number of times interest changed

$= 3 \times 4 = 12$ times [$\because$ 1 yr = 4 quarters]

7. *(a)* Let sum borrowed be P.

Amount paid = 2 × ₹ 882 = ₹ 1764

Time = 2 yr, $r = 5\%$

Using compound interest formula,

$$\text{Amount} = P\left[1 + \frac{R}{100}\right]^n \Rightarrow 1764 = P\left[1 + \frac{5}{100}\right]^2$$

$$\Rightarrow \quad P = \frac{1764}{\left(\frac{21}{20}\right)^2} = \frac{1764 \times 400}{441} = 1600$$

$\therefore$ Amount borrowed was ₹ 1600.

8. *(b)* Present population

$$= 160000\left(1 + \frac{3}{100}\right)\left(1 + \frac{2 \cdot 5}{100}\right)\left(1 + \frac{5}{100}\right)$$

$$= 160000 \times \frac{103}{100} \times \frac{102 \cdot 5}{100} \times \frac{105}{100} = 177366$$

9. *(a)* Given, $r = 5\%$, $T = 2$ yr

Total amount paid after 2 yr

= ₹(5000 + 3820) = ₹ 8820, $P = ?$

$$\text{We know Amount} = P\left[1 + \frac{R}{100}\right]^n$$

$$\therefore \quad 8820 = P\left[1 + \frac{5}{100}\right]^2$$

$$\Rightarrow \quad P = \frac{8820}{\left(\frac{21}{20}\right)^2} \Rightarrow P = \frac{8820 \times 400}{441}$$

$$\Rightarrow \quad P = ₹\, 8000$$

10. (b) $A = P\left(1+\frac{r_1}{100}\right)\left(1+\frac{r_2}{100}\right)\left(1+\frac{r_3}{100}\right)$

$\Rightarrow A = 10000\left(1+\frac{4}{100}\right)\left(1+\frac{5}{100}\right)\left(1+\frac{6}{100}\right)$

$= 10000 \times \frac{104}{100} \times \frac{105}{100} \times \frac{106}{100}$

$=$ ₹11575.20

$\therefore$ CI = ₹11575.20 − ₹10000 = ₹1575.20

11. (b) Given, r for Ist year = 10%

r for IInd year = 20%

r for IIIrd year = 20%

$\therefore$ After 3 yr total population will be

$= 8000\left(1+\frac{10}{100}\right)\left(1+\frac{20}{100}\right)\left(1-\frac{20}{100}\right)$

$= 8000 \times \frac{11}{10} \times \frac{12}{10} \times \frac{8}{10} = 8448$

12. (d) Given, $P =$ ₹ 8000

$t = 3$ yr; $r = 10\%$

As we know, $A = P\left(1+\frac{r}{100}\right)^t$

$= 8000\left[1+\frac{10}{100}\right]^3 = 8000\left[\frac{11}{10}\right]^3$

$= 8000 \times \frac{11}{10} \times \frac{11}{10} \times \frac{11}{10} =$ ₹ 10648

13. (c) Let the principal be P in case of SI.

$r = r\%$, $T = 2$ yr, amount, A = 2P

SI = A − P = 2P − P = P

$\therefore \quad P = \frac{P \times r \times 2}{100} \qquad \left[\because \text{SI} = \frac{PRT}{100}\right]$

$\Rightarrow \quad r = 50\%$

In case of compound interest,

$r = R\%$, $t = 2$ yr, A = 2P

Using formula, $A = P\left[1+\frac{r}{100}\right]^t$

$\therefore \quad 2P = P\left[1+\frac{R}{100}\right]^2 \Rightarrow 2 = \left(1+\frac{R}{100}\right)^2$

$\Rightarrow 1 + \frac{R}{100} = \sqrt{2} = 1.41$

$\Rightarrow R = 0.41 \times 100 = 41\%$ i.e. $r > R$

14. (a) Interest paid by Mehak

$= \frac{62500 \times 2 \times 4}{100} =$ ₹ 5000

$[\because P = 62500, r = 2\%, t = 4]$

But, in case of Monisha,

$P = 60000$, $r = 4\%$, $t = 2$ yr

$\therefore \quad A = 60000 \times \left(1+\frac{4}{100}\right)^2$

$= 60000 \times \frac{104 \times 104}{10000} = 64896$

Interest paid = 64896 − 60000 = 4896

$\therefore$ Mehak paid more interest by

= 5000 − 4896 = ₹104

15. (a) I. False II. False III. True IV. False

SI = A − P = 1331 − 1000 = 331

$\because \text{SI} = \frac{P \times R \times T}{100} \Rightarrow 331 = \frac{1000 \times R \times 3}{100}$

$\Rightarrow R = \frac{331}{30} = 11.03\%$

16. (b) I. SI = CI for $T = 1$ yr

II. $A = P\left(1+\frac{r}{100}\right)^n$

III. $\text{SI} = \frac{PRT}{100} \Rightarrow 40 = \frac{500 \times 10 \times T}{100} \Rightarrow T = \frac{4}{5}$ yr

IV. If CI is calculate on half yearly, then for 2 yr, then = 4

17. (c) Let amount at 5% be ₹x.

$\therefore$ Amount at 8% = ₹ (1550 − x)

In SI case,

$\frac{x \times 5 \times 3}{100} + \frac{(1550 - x) \times 8 \times 3}{100} = 300$

$\Rightarrow 15x + 1550 \times 24 - 24x = 300 \times 100$

$\Rightarrow \quad 37200 - 30000 = 9x$

$\Rightarrow \quad 7200 = 9x \Rightarrow x = 800$

$\therefore$ Amount lent at 5% = ₹800

Now, amount lent at 8% = ₹(1550 − 800) = 750

$\therefore$ Required ratio $= \frac{800}{750} = 16:15$

18. (a) n is the simple interest on m.

p is the simple interest on n.

Let time be t and rate be r.

For both cases,

$n = \frac{m \times r \times t}{100}$

$\Rightarrow \quad \frac{r \times t}{100} = \frac{n}{m} \qquad \ldots(i)$

Again, $\quad p = \frac{n \times r \times t}{100}$

$\Rightarrow \quad \frac{r \times t}{100} = \frac{p}{n} \qquad \ldots(ii)$

From Eqs. (i) and (ii), we get

$\frac{n}{m} = \frac{p}{n} \Rightarrow n^2 = mp$

19. (c) Let the sum be ₹ 100. Then,

$$SI = ₹\frac{100 \times 2 \times 8}{100} = ₹16$$

$$CI = ₹100\left[\left(1+\frac{8}{100}\right)^2 - 1\right]$$

$$= ₹100\left[\left(\frac{27}{25}\right)^2 - 1\right]$$

$$= ₹100 \times \left[\frac{729-625}{625}\right]$$

$$= \left(\frac{100 \times 104}{625}\right) = ₹16.64$$

∴ Difference = ₹ 0.64

If difference between CI and SI is ₹0.64, sum = ₹ 100

If the difference is ₹ 768, Sum

$$= ₹\left(\frac{100}{0.64} \times 768\right) = ₹120000$$

20. (a) Given $3P = P\left(1+\frac{r}{100}\right)^3$

$$\Rightarrow \left(1+\frac{r}{100}\right)^3 = 3 \quad \text{... (i)}$$

Let t be the time in years in which the sum will be nine time of itself. Then,

$$9P = P\left(1+\frac{r}{100}\right)^t$$

$$\Rightarrow \left(1+\frac{r}{100}\right)^t = 9 = 3^2$$

$$\Rightarrow \left(1+\frac{r}{100}\right)^t = \left[\left(1+\frac{r}{100}\right)^3\right]^2 \quad \text{[from Eq. (i)]}$$

$$\Rightarrow \left(1+\frac{r}{100}\right)^t = \left(1+\frac{r}{100}\right)^6 \quad \text{[on comparing]}$$

$$\Rightarrow t = 6 \text{ yr}$$

21. (b) Given, CI = ₹ 420, $r = 10\%$, $t = 2$ yr

$$\because \quad CI = P\left[\left(1+\frac{r}{100}\right)^t - 1\right]$$

$$\Rightarrow 420 = P\left[\left(1+\frac{10}{100}\right)^2 - 1\right] = P\left[\frac{121}{100} - 1\right]$$

$$\Rightarrow 420 = P \times \frac{21}{100}$$

$$\Rightarrow P = ₹\ 2000$$

Now, t = double = 4 yr

r = half = 5%

$$SI = \frac{P \times R \times T}{100} = \frac{2000 \times 5 \times 4}{100} = ₹\ 400$$

22. (a) I. Given, $P = 10500$

$R\% = 5\%$ per annum, $T = 3$ yr

$$CI = P\left[\left(1+\frac{R}{100}\right)^n - 1\right]$$

$$CI = 10500\left[\left(1+\frac{5}{10}\right)^3 - 1\right]$$

$$= 10500\left[\frac{105 \times 105 \times 105}{100 \times 100 \times 100} - 1\right]$$

$$= 10500\left[\frac{1157625 - 1000000}{1000000}\right]$$

$$= \frac{10500 \times 157625}{1000000} = 1655.06$$

II. $r = \frac{R\%}{4} = \frac{10\%}{4} = 2.25\%$

III. $A = P\left(1+\frac{r/2}{100}\right)^n$

IV. CI > SI

Chapter 10 : Alegebraic Expressions

1. (b)
$$\begin{array}{r} 5x^2 + 3x - 8 \\ + 4x^2 - 5x + 6 \\ \hline 9x^2 - 2x - 2 \end{array}$$

2. (c) We have, $P = -2y^2 + \frac{1}{2}y - 3$

and $Q = 7y^2 - 2y + 10$

Now, $(Q - P)$

$$\begin{array}{r} 7y^2 - 2y + 10 \\ -2y^2 + \frac{1}{2}y - 3 \\ (+) \quad (-) \quad (+) \\ \hline 9y^2 - \frac{5}{2}y + 13 \end{array}$$

The value of $(Q - P)$ is $= 9y^2 - \frac{5}{2}y + 13$

3. (c) $g(x) + 2g(x) = 3g(x)$ is true statement.

4. (b) $6x^2 + 6y + 9x^2 - 3y + 2x - 5x^2$

$= 10x^2 + 3y + 2x$

LHS $= 6x^2 + 6y + 9x^2 - 3y + 2x - 5x^2$

$= 6x^2 + 9x^2 - 5x^2 + 6y - 3y + 2x$

$= 10x^2 + 3y + 2x =$ RHS

5. (c) Given, $A = (7xy + 5y)$ and $B = 3xy$

$A \times B = (7xy + 5y) \times 3xy$

$= 7xy \times 3xy + 5y \times 3xy$

$= 21x^{1+1}y^{1+1} + 15xy^{1+1} = 21x^2y^2 + 15xy^2$

6. (a) Required sum

$= a - b + ab + b + c - bc + c - a - ac$

$= 2c + ab - bc - ac$

7. (a) Let A be added

$x^3 + x^2 + x - 1 + A = x^4 + 2x^2 - 3x + 7$

$\Rightarrow \quad A = x^4 + 2x^2 - 3x + 7 - (x^3 + x^2 + x - 1)$

$\Rightarrow \quad A = x^4 + 2x^2 - 3x + 7 - x^3 - x^2 - x + 1$

$\Rightarrow \quad A = x^4 - x^3 + x^2 - 4x + 8$

8. (a) Let length of a rectangle, $l = x$ m

Then, breadth of rectangle, $b = (2x - 5)$ m

$\therefore$ Perimeter $= 2(l + b) = 2(x + 2x - 5)$

$= 2(3x - 5) = 6x - 10$

9. (b) Length of rectangle $= x$

$\therefore$ Breadth of rectangle $= (x - 4)$

$\therefore$ Area of rectangle = Length × breadth

$= x.(x - 4) = x^2 - 4x$

10. (b) $(x^2 + 3x + 5) \times (x^2 - 1)$

$= x^2 (x^2 + 3x + 5) - 1 (x^2 + 3x + 5)$

$= x^4 + 3x^3 + 5x^2 - x^2 - 3x - 5$

$= x^4 + 3x^3 + 4x^2 - 3x - 5$

11. (a) $? = \left(\frac{x}{2} - \frac{3y}{4}\right)\left(\frac{5x}{4} - \frac{y}{2}\right)$

$= \frac{5x}{4}\left(\frac{x}{2} - \frac{3y}{4}\right) - \frac{y}{2}\left(\frac{x}{2} - \frac{3y}{4}\right)$

$= \frac{5x^2}{8} - \frac{15xy}{16} - \frac{xy}{4} + \frac{3y^2}{8} = \frac{5x^2}{8} - \frac{19xy}{16} + \frac{3y^2}{8}$

12. (a) Area of rectangle $= x^2 + 7x + 12$

Breadth = ?

Length $= (x + 3)$

We know that,

Area of rectangle = Length × Breadth

$(x^2 + 7x + 12) = (x + 3) \times$ Breadth

$\Rightarrow (x^2 + 7x + 12) \div (x + 3) =$ Breadth

$\Rightarrow (x + 4)(x + 3) \div (x + 3) =$ Breadth

$\Rightarrow \quad x + 4 =$ Breadth

$\therefore$ Breadth $= 2 + 4 = 6$ $\quad [\because x = 2$, given$]$

13. (d) $\frac{6 \times 6 - 1.5 \times 1.5}{4.5} = a + b$

$\frac{(6)^2 - (1.5)^2}{(6 - 1.5)} = a + b$

$\Rightarrow \quad \frac{(6 + 1.5)(6 - 1.5)}{(6 - 1.5)} = a + b$

$[\because a^2 - b^2 = (a + b)(a - b)]$

$6 + 1.5 = a + b$

$\therefore \quad a = 6$

14. (b) $n^4 - 10n^3 + 36n^2 - 49n + 24$ at $n = 1$

$= (1)^4 - 10 \times (1)^3 + 36 \times (1)^2 - 49 \times 1 + 24$

[on putting $n = 1$]

$= 1 - 10 + 36 - 49 + 24 = 61 - 59 = 2$

15. (b) $6m^2 - 9mn - 3m - 20 = -2$

LHS $6m^2 - 9mn - 3m - 20$

At $m = 3, n = 1$

LHS $= 6 \times 3^2 - 9 \times 3 \times 1 - 3 \times 3 - 20$

$= 6 \times 9 - 27 - 9 - 20$

$= 54 - 27 - 29 = 27 - 29 = -2$

= RHS

16. (c) $\frac{2x^3 - 12x^2 + 16x}{(x - 2)(x - 4)} = \frac{2x(x^2 - 6x + 8)}{x^2 - 6x + 8} = 2x$

17. (b) Required value $\left(2 + \frac{4}{x}\right)\left(10 - \frac{15}{x} + \frac{25}{x^2}\right)$

$= (2 + 4)(10 - 15 + 25)$ $\quad [\because x = 1]$

$= (6)(20) = 120$

18. (b) Perimeter of the triangle $= 8p^2 - 9p + 9$

$\therefore$ Perimeter of a triangle = Sum of the length of all three sides

i.e. length of first side + length of second side + length of third side

So, $8p^2 - 9p + 9 = 2p^2 - 3p + 1 + 5p^2 - p + 4 +$ Length of third side

$\Rightarrow$ Length of third side

$= 8p^2 - 9p + 9 - (7p^2 - 4p + 5)$

$= 8p^2 - 9p + 9 - 7p^2 + 4p - 5$

$= p^2 - 5p + 4$

19. (d) Given $x = pq$ and $p = q = 4$

On putting the value in algebraic expression

$8 \times (4)^3 + 6(pq)^2 + 9 \times 4 \times 4 - 8 \times pq \times pq$

$= 8 \times 64 + 6(pq)^2 + 9 \times 16 - 8(pq)^2$

$= 8 \times 64 + 6(pq)^2 - 8(pq)^2 + 9 \times 16$

$= 512 - 2(pq)^2 + 144$

$= 512 - 2(16)^2 + 144$

$= 512 - 2 \times 256 + 144$

$= 512 - 512 + 144 = 144$

20. (c) $\frac{6p^3 - 36p^2 + 48p}{(p - 2)(p - 4)}$

$= \frac{6p(p^2 - 6p + 8)}{p^2 - 4p - 2p + 8}$

$= \frac{6p(p^2 - 6p + 8)}{p^2 - 6p + 8}$

$= 6p$ $\quad [\therefore$ given $p = 8]$

Put $p = 8$

$= 6 \times 8 = 48$

21. (b) Given,

$2x + 3y = 6\sqrt{3}$ ...(i)

$2x - 3y = 6$ ...(ii)

On adding Eqs. (i) and (ii),

$4x + 0 = 6\sqrt{3} + 6$

$\Rightarrow \quad 4x = 6(\sqrt{3} + 1)$

$\Rightarrow \quad x = \frac{6}{4}(\sqrt{3} + 1)$

$\Rightarrow \quad x = \frac{3}{2}(\sqrt{3} + 1)$

Similarly subtract Eq. (ii) from Eq. (i),

$2x + 3y = 6\sqrt{3}$

$2x - 3y = 6$

$- \quad (+) \quad (-)$

$6y = 6\sqrt{3} - 6$

$\Rightarrow \quad 6y = 6(\sqrt{3} - 1)$

$\Rightarrow \quad y = \sqrt{3} - 1$

22. (a) Given equations are

$2x + 3y = 23$ ...(i)

$2x - 3y = 5$ ...(ii)

On adding Eqs. (i) and (ii), we get

$4x = 28 \Rightarrow x = 7$

On subtracting Eq. (ii) from Eq. (i), we get

$6y = 18 \Rightarrow y = 3$

Put the value of $x = 7$ and $y = 3$ in given expression.

$\therefore \frac{2x^2 + 3x + 1}{4y^2 - 9y + 31} = \frac{2 \times 49 + 3 \times 7 + 1}{4 \times 9 - 9 \times 3 + 31}$

$= \frac{98 + 21 + 1}{36 - 27 + 31}$

$= \frac{120}{40} = 3$

23. (b) $(x^2 + xy - y^2)(x^2 - xy + y^2)$

$= x^2(x^2 - xy + y^2) + xy(x^2 - xy + y^2) - y^2(x^2 - xy + y^2)$

$= x^4 - x^3y + x^2y^2 + x^3y - x^2y^2 + xy^3 - y^2x^2 + xy^3 - y^4$

$= x^4 + 2xy^3 - x^2y^2 - y^4$

Let the algebraic expression to be added be A. Then,

$A = x^2y^2 - (x^4 + 2xy^3 - x^2y^2 - y^4)$

$= x^2y^2 - x^4 - 2xy^3 + x^2y^2 + y^4$

$= 2x^2y^2 - x^4 - 2xy^3 + y^4$

24. (a) I. LHS $= (x - y) \times (3x + 5y)$

$= x \times (3x + 5y) - y \times (3x + 5y)$

$= (x \times 3x) + (x \times 5y) - (y \times 3x) - (y \times 5y)$

$= 3x^2 + 5xy - 3yx - 5y^2$

$= 3x^2 + 2xy - 5y^2$

II. $(x + a)(x + b) = x^2 + (a + b)x + ab$

III. $a^2 + b^2 + c^2 - ab - bc - ca$

$= a^2 + a^2 + a^2 - a \cdot a - a \cdot a - a \cdot a$

$= 3a^2 - 3a^2 = 0$

IV. LHS $= 3y(2y - 7) - 3(y - 4) - 63$

$= 6y^2 - 21y - 3y + 12 - 63$

$= 6y^2 - 24y - 51$

For $y = -2$,

$6y^2 - 24y - 51 = 6(-2)^2 - 24(-2) - 51$

$= 6 \times 4 + 24 \times 2 - 51$

$= 24 + 48 - 51$

$= 72 - 51 = 21$

V. Here, the given exbression is $x^2 + 4xz + 4x^2$

$\Rightarrow \quad (4)z^2 + (4x)z + x^2$

So, coefficeint of $z^2 = 4$

25. (a) I. True, $(2x + y)^2 + (6x^2 + 3y^2 - 4xy)$

$= 4x^2 + y^2 + 4xy + 6x^2 + 3y^2 - 4xy$

$= 10x^2 + 4y^2$

II. False, $\frac{x/4}{4/x} = \frac{x^2}{16} \neq 1$

III. False, $(5x - 63) \div 9 = \frac{5x - 63}{9} = \frac{5}{9}x - 7$

IV. True,

$64^2 - 56^2 = 120p$

$\Rightarrow \quad (64 + 56)(64 - 56) = 120p$

$\Rightarrow \quad 120 \times 8 = 120p$

$\therefore \quad p = 8$

26. (b) I. First expression $= 5m(3 - m)$

$= (5m \times 3) - (5m \times m)$

$= 15m - 5m^2$

Now adding the second expression to it,

$15m - 5m^2 + 6m^2 - 13m = m^2 + 2m$

II. $(x + a)(x + b) = x^2 + (a + b)x + ab$

$\because a = 2, b = 3$ [given]

$= x^2 + (2 + 3)x + 2 \times 3 = x^2 + 5x + 6$

III. $34 \times 26 = (30 + 4)(30 - 4)$

$\Rightarrow (a + b)(a - b)$ or $(x + b)(x - b)$

IV. First expression

$= 4m(3m^2 + 5m - 7)$

$= (4m \times 3m^2) + (4m \times 5m) + (4m \times (-7))$

$= 12m^3 + 20m^2 - 28m$

The second expression $= 2(m^3 - 4m^2 + 5)$

$= 2m^3 + 2 \times (-4m^2) + 2 \times 5$

$= 2m^3 - 8m^2 + 10$

Adding the two expressions,

$(12m^3 + 20m^2 - 28m) + (2m^3 - 8m^2 + 10)$

$= 14m^3 + 12m^2 - 28m + 10$

Chapter 11 : Factorisation of Algebraic Expressions

1. (a) $17ab - 68ab^2 = 17ab - 2 \times 2 \times 17ab^2$
$= 17ab(1 - 4b)$

2. (a) $xy - pq + qy - px = xy - px - pq + qy$
$= x(y - p) + q(-p + y)$
$= x(y - p) + q(y - p) = (x + q)(y - p)$

3. (d) $6 - y - 2y^2 = -(2y^2 + y - 6)$
$= -(2y^2 + 4y - 3y - 6)$
$= -\{2y(y + 2) - 3(y + 2)\}$
$= -\{(2y - 3)(y + 2)\}$
$= (y + 2)(-2y + 3)$

4. (d) I. $x^2 - 13x + 42$
II. $x^2 - 7x - 6x + 42$
III. $x(x - 7) - 6(x - 7)$
IV. $(x - 7)(x - 6)$
$\therefore$ Step III is incorrect.

5. (c) Given, cost of 1 shirt is ₹ $(2x^2 - 4x - 10)$
$\therefore$ The cost of $(x + 2)$ shirts is $(2x^2 - 4x - 10)(x + 2)$
$= x(2x^2 - 4x - 10) + 2(2x^2 - 4x - 10)$
$= 2x^3 - 4x^2 - 10x + 4x^2 - 8x - 20$
$= 2x^3 - 18x - 20$

6. (b) $10x^2 + 21x + 9 = (2x + 3)(5x + 3)$
Put $x = 10$ in both sides, we get
$10 \cdot (10)^2 + 21 \cdot (10) + 9 = (2 \times 10 + 3)(5 \times 10 + 3)$
$\Rightarrow \quad 1000 + 210 + 9 = 23 \times 53$
$\Rightarrow \quad 1219 = 23 \times 53$

7. (a) $2x^2 - \frac{5}{6}x + \frac{1}{12}$
$= \frac{24x^2 - 10x + 1}{12}$
$= \frac{1}{12}(24x^2 - 10x + 1)$
$= \frac{1}{12}(24x^2 - 6x - 4x + 1)$
$= \frac{1}{12}\{6x(4x - 1) - 1(4x - 1)\}$
$= \frac{1}{12}(6x - 1)(4x - 1) = \left(\frac{x}{2} - \frac{1}{12}\right)(4x - 1)$

8. (b) LHS $= 6x^2 + 19x + 8$
$= 6x^2 + 19x + 3 + 5$
$= (6x^2 + 19x + 3) + 5$
$= [6x^2 + 18x + x + 3] + 5$
$= [6x(x + 3) + 1(x + 3)] + 5$
$= [(x + 3)(6x + 1)] + 5 = (6x + 1)(x + 3) + 5$
And RHS $= A(x + 3) + 5$
On comparing LHS from RHS, we get
$A = (6x + 1)$

9. (c) $(x^2 - 5x)(x^2 - 5x - 20) + 84$
$= (x^2 - 5x)(x^2 - 5x) - 20(x^2 - 5x) + 84$
$= (x^2 - 5x)^2 - 20(x^2 - 5x) + 84$
Let $x^2 - 5x = a$
Then, the given expression
$= a^2 - 20a + 84$
$= a^2 - 6a - 14a + 84$
$= a(a - 6) - 14(a - 6) = (a - 6)(a - 14)$
$= (x^2 - 5x - 6)(x^2 - 5x - 14)$
$= (x^2 - 6x + x - 6)(x^2 - 7x + 2x - 14)$
$= [x(x - 6) + 1(x - 6)][x(x - 7) + 2(x - 7)]$
$= (x - 6)(x + 1)(x - 7)(x + 2)$
Hence, $(x - 7)$ is one of the factor of given expression.

10. (c) $x^2 + \frac{1}{x^2} + 2 - 2x - \frac{2}{x}$
$= x^2 + \frac{1}{x^2} + 1 + 1 - 2x - \frac{2}{x}$
$= x^2 + 1 + \frac{1}{x^2} + 1 - 2x - \frac{2}{x}$
$= x\left(x + \frac{1}{x}\right) + \frac{1}{x^2} + 1 - 2\left(x + \frac{1}{x}\right)$
$= x\left(x + \frac{1}{x}\right) + \frac{1}{x}\left(x + \frac{1}{x}\right) - 2\left(x + \frac{1}{x}\right)$
$= \left(x + \frac{1}{x}\right)\left(x + \frac{1}{x} - 2\right)$

11. (d) LHS $= x^8 - x^4 - 72$
Let $x^4 = a$. Then,
$x^8 - x^4 - 72 = a^2 - a - 72$
$= a^2 - 9a + 8a - 72$
$= a(a - 9) + 8(a - 9)$
$= (a - 9)(a + 8)$
$= (x^4 - 9)(x^4 + 8)$
$\therefore$ RHS $= (x^4 - A)(x^4 + B)$
On compairing LHS and RHS, we get
$A = 9, B = 8$

12. (b) The given factorisation shows that the method of algebraic identity is being used.
i.e. $a^2 + 2ab + b^2 = (a + b)^2 = (a + b)(a + b)$

13. (b) $y^2 + 18y + 65 = ay^2 + 2by + 65$
On comparing, we get
$a = 1, 2b = 18$

$\Rightarrow \quad b = 9$

$\therefore \quad \dfrac{a+b}{a-b} = \dfrac{1+9}{1-9} = -\dfrac{10}{8} = -\dfrac{5}{4}$

14. (c) Quotient of $(x^3y^3 + x^2y^3 - xy^4 + xy) \div xy$

$= (x^2y^2 + xy^2 - y^3 + 1)\, xy \div xy$

$= x^2y^2 + xy^2 - y^3 + 1$

Now, factors of quotient

$= xy^2(x+1) - (y^3 - 1)$

$= xy^2(x+1) - (y-1)(y^2 + y + 1)$

So, we can't factorise.

15. (d) First expression

$(5x-3)^2 - (5x-3) - 20$

Let $(5x-3) = a$

Then, the expression becomes

$a^2 - a - 20 = a^2 - 5a + 4a - 20$

$= a(a-5) + 4(a-5) = (a-5)(a+4)$

$= (5x - 3 - 5)(5x - 3 + 4)$

$= (5x-8)(5x+1)$

Now given expression

$[(5x-3)^2 - (5x-3) - 20] \div (5x-8)$

$= \dfrac{(5x-8)(5x+1)}{(5x-8)} = 5x+1$

16. (a) A. $x^2 - 4x + 4$

$= x^2 - 2x - 2x + 4$

$= x(x-2) - 2(x-2)$ [write $-4x = -2x - 2x$]

$= (x-2)(x-2)$

$= (x-2)^2$ $[\because a \cdot a = a^2]$

Perfect square

B. $x^2 - 5x + 6 = x^2 - 3x - 2x + 6$

$= x(x-3) - 2(x-3)$

$= (x-3)(x-2)$

C. $x^2 - 9x + 18 = x^2 - 6x - 3x + 18$

$= x(x-6) - 3(x-6)$

$= (x-6)(x-3)$

D. $3x^2 - 24x + 36 = 3\{x^2 - 8x + 12\}$

$= 3\{x^2 - 6x - 2x + 12\}$

$= 3\{x(x-6) - 2(x-6)\}$

$= 3\{(x-6)(x-2)\}$

Except (A), all (rest) three are factorised by splitting the middle term.

17. (a) Given,

Length of rectangle = 32 units

Breadth of rectangle = 18 units

Area of Rectangle = Length × Breadth

$= 32 \times 18 = 576$ sq unit

$\therefore$ Given : Area of rectangle = Area of square.

Side of square $= 5x + 4$

Area of square = (Side × Side)

$= (5x+4)(5x+4) = 576$

$\Rightarrow \quad (5x+4)^2 = 576$

Taking square root

$5x + 4 = 24 \Rightarrow 5x = 24 - 4$

$\Rightarrow \quad 5x = 20 \Rightarrow x = 4$

18. (b) $\dfrac{6 \times 1.5 \times 1.5 + 1.5 \times 18 + 1.5 + 3}{2 \times 1.5 \times 1.5 - 8 \times 1.5 + 5 \times 1.5 - 20}$

$= \dfrac{(6 \times 1.5)(1.5 + 3) + 1(1.5 + 3)}{(2 \times 1.5)(1.5 - 4) + 5(1.5 - 4)}$

$= \dfrac{(1.5 + 3)(6 \times 1.5 + 1)}{(1.5 - 4)(2 \times 1.5 + 5)}$

$= \dfrac{4.5(9+1)}{2.5(3+5)} = \dfrac{4.5 \times 10}{2.5 \times 8}$

$= \dfrac{45}{20} = \dfrac{9}{4} = 2\dfrac{1}{4}$

19. (b) I. $8x^2 - 18x + 9 = 8x^2 - 12x - 6x + 9$

$= 4x(2x-3) - 3(2x-3)$

$= (4x-3) \times (2x-3)$

II. $x^2 - 12 - x$

$= x^2 - x - 12$

$= x^2 - 4x + 3x - 12$

$= x(x-4) + 3(x-4)$

$= (x-4)(x+3)$

III. Area of a square $= (\text{side})^2 = 625\,\text{cm}^2$

$\Rightarrow \quad (7x - 24)^2 = 625$

$\Rightarrow \quad (7x-24)^2 = (25)^2$

Taking square root on both side,

$7x - 24 = 25$

$\Rightarrow 7x = 25 + 24 = 49$

$\Rightarrow \quad x = 7$

IV. LHS $x^2 + 10x + 16$

$= x^2 + 8x + 2x + 16$

$= x(x+8) + 2(x+8)$

$= (x+8)(x+2)$

$\therefore$ RHS $= (x+8)(x+p)$

On comparing LHS and RHS, we get $p = 2$.

Chapter 12 : Linear Equations in One Variable

1. (a) Let the linear equations in one variable be
$2x = 6, y + 5 = 10, \ldots$
Here, maximum power of variable must be 1.

2. (d) $(1 + x)$ is a linear expression.

3. (a) $(2x - 2)^2 = 4x^2 + 4x - 4$
$\Rightarrow \quad 4x^2 - 8x + 4 = 4x^2 + 4x - 4$
$\Rightarrow \quad -8x + 4 = 4x - 4 \Rightarrow 12x = 8$
which is linear equation in one variable.

4. (b) $\dfrac{3x-1}{3x+1} = \dfrac{2x+3}{2x-1}$
$\Rightarrow \quad (3x-1)(2x-1) = (2x+3)(3x+1)$
$\Rightarrow 6x^2 - 3x - 2x + 1 = 6x^2 + 2x + 9x + 3$
$\Rightarrow \quad -5x + 1 = 11x + 3$
$\Rightarrow \quad 11x + 3 = -5x + 1$
$\Rightarrow \quad 16x = 1 - 3 \Rightarrow x = \dfrac{-2}{16}$
$x = \dfrac{-1}{8}$

5. (c) $\dfrac{6x+1}{3} + 1 = \dfrac{x-3}{6}$
Multiplying both sides of the equation by 6
$\dfrac{6(6x+1)}{3} + 6 \times 1 = \dfrac{6(x-3)}{6}$
$\Rightarrow \quad 2(6x+1) + 6 = x - 3$
$\Rightarrow \quad 12x + 2 + 6 = x - 3$
$\Rightarrow \quad 12x + 8 = x - 3$
$\Rightarrow \quad 12x + 8 - x = -3$
$\Rightarrow \quad 11x + 8 = -3$

6. (a) We have, $3x + 2(x + 5) = 75$
$\Rightarrow \quad 3x + 2x + 10 = 75 \Rightarrow 5x = 65$
$\therefore \quad x = 13$

7. (a) From option (a), $3y + 2 = 4y + 2$
$\Rightarrow \quad 4y - 3y = 2 - 2 \Rightarrow y = 0$, is neither an odd nor an even.

8. (c) From option (a), $6x - 3 = 3x - 5 \Rightarrow 3x = -2$
$\therefore \quad x = -\dfrac{2}{3}$
From option (b), $x - 3 = x + 4$, No solution.
From option (c), $5x - 3 = 3x - 7 \Rightarrow 2x = -4$
$\therefore \quad x = -2$
From option (d), $7x - 6 = 6x - 5 \Rightarrow x = 1$

9. (b) $\because \dfrac{a-8}{5} = \dfrac{a-6}{3}$ [given]
$\Rightarrow 3a - 24 = 5a - 30 \Rightarrow 2a = 6$
$\therefore \quad a = 3$

10. (b) Given equation is
$\dfrac{x}{3} - \dfrac{1}{4}\left(x - \dfrac{1}{2}\right) = \dfrac{1}{8}(x+1) + \dfrac{1}{12}$
$\Rightarrow \quad \dfrac{x}{3} - \dfrac{x}{4} + \dfrac{1}{8} = \dfrac{1}{8}x + \dfrac{1}{8} + \dfrac{1}{12}$
$\Rightarrow \quad \dfrac{x}{3} - \dfrac{x}{4} - \dfrac{x}{8} = \dfrac{1}{12}$
$\Rightarrow \quad \dfrac{8x - 6x - 3x}{24} = \dfrac{1}{12}$
$\Rightarrow \quad \dfrac{-x}{24} = \dfrac{1}{12}$
$\therefore \quad x = -2$

11. (d) $\dfrac{x+23}{5} + 5(x-3) = \dfrac{x+3}{2} + 3x$
Multiplying both sides of the equation by LCM = 10, we get
$\dfrac{10(x+23)}{5} + 10 \times 5(x-3) = \dfrac{10(x+3)}{2} + 10 \times 3x$
$\Rightarrow \quad 2(x+23) + 50(x-3) = 5(x+3) + 30x$
$\Rightarrow \quad 2x + 46 + 50x - 150 = 5x + 15 + 30x$
$\Rightarrow \quad 2x + 50x - 5x - 30x = 15 - 46 + 150$
$\Rightarrow \quad 17x = 119$
$\Rightarrow \quad x = 7$

12. (d) $0.18(5y - 4) = 0.5y + 0.8$
$\Rightarrow 0.18 \times 5y - 0.18 \times 4 = 0.5y + 0.8$
$\Rightarrow \quad 0.90y - 0.72 = 0.5y + 0.8$
$\Rightarrow \quad 0.90y - 0.5y = 0.8 + 0.72$
[Collecting variables and numbers]
$\Rightarrow \quad 0.4y + 1.52$
$\Rightarrow \quad y = \dfrac{1.52}{0.4}$
$\Rightarrow \quad y = \dfrac{152}{40}$
$\Rightarrow \quad y = 3.8$

13. (c) $\dfrac{(x^2 - 5x + 6)}{(x^2 - 7x + 12)} = \dfrac{(x^2 - x - 6)}{(x^2 + 7x + 10)}$
$\Rightarrow \quad \dfrac{x^2 - 3x - 2x + 6}{x^2 - 3x - 4x + 12} = \dfrac{x^2 - 3x + 2x - 6}{x^2 + 5x + 2x + 10}$
$\Rightarrow \dfrac{x(x-3) - 2(x-3)}{x(x-3) - 4(x-3)} = \dfrac{x(x-3) + 2(x-3)}{x(x+5) + 2(x+5)}$
$\Rightarrow \quad \dfrac{(x-3)(x-2)}{(x-3)(x-4)} = \dfrac{(x-3)(x+2)}{(x+5)(x+2)}$
$\Rightarrow \quad \dfrac{x-2}{x-4} = \dfrac{x-3}{x+5}$
$\Rightarrow \quad (x-2)(x+5) = (x-3)(x-4)$
$\Rightarrow \quad x^2 + 3x - 10 = x^2 - 7x + 12$
$\Rightarrow \quad 3x + 7x = 12 + 10$
$\Rightarrow \quad 10x = 22$
$\Rightarrow \quad x = 2.2$ or $x = 2.20$

14. (c) We have, $\frac{3t-2}{4}-\frac{2t+3}{3}=\frac{2}{3}-t$

Multiplying both side of the equation by LCM $=12$

$\Rightarrow \frac{12(3t-2)}{4}-\frac{12(2t+3)}{3}=12\times\frac{2}{3}-12\times t$

$\Rightarrow 3(3t-2)-4(2t+3)=4\times 2-12t$

$\Rightarrow 9t-6-8t-12=8-12t$

$\Rightarrow 9t-8t+12t=8+6+12$

$\Rightarrow 13t=26$ [collecting variables and numbers]

$\Rightarrow t=2$

15. (b) Given $0.3y+0.4=0.28y+1.16$

$\Rightarrow 0.30y-0.28y=1.16-0.40$

$\Rightarrow 0.02y=0.76$

$\Rightarrow y=\frac{0.76}{0.02}=38$

$\Rightarrow y=38$

Now, the value of $\frac{2y+24}{0.5y+101}$ at $y=38$

On putting $y=38$, we get $\frac{2\times 38+24}{0.5\times 38+101}$

$=\frac{76+24}{19+101}=\frac{100}{120}=\frac{5}{6}$

16. (b) Given,

$$\frac{6x^2+13x-4}{2x+5}=\frac{12x^2+5x-2}{4x+3}$$

$\Rightarrow (4x+3)(6x^2+13x-4)$

$=(2x+5)(12x^2+5x-2)$

$\Rightarrow 24x^3+52x^2-16x+18x^2+39x-12$

$=24x^3+10x^2-4x+60x^2+25x-10$

$\Rightarrow 24x^3+70x^2-16x+39x-12$

$-24x^3-70x^2-21x+10=0$

$\Rightarrow 23x-12-21x+10=0$

$\Rightarrow 23x-21x=-10+12$

$\Rightarrow 2x=2$

$\Rightarrow x=1$

On putting $x=1$ in $\frac{2x^2+3x+2}{5x+7}$, we get

$\frac{2\times 1+3+2}{5\times 1+7}=\frac{7}{12}$

17. (b) Given, $\frac{2}{5}(4x-1)-\left[4x-\left(\frac{1-3x}{2}\right)\right]=\frac{x-7}{2}$

$\Rightarrow \frac{8x-2}{5}-\left[\frac{8x-1+3x}{2}\right]=\frac{x-7}{2}$

$\Rightarrow \frac{8x-2}{5}-\frac{11x-1}{2}=\frac{x-7}{2}$

$\Rightarrow \frac{16x-4-55x+5}{10}=\frac{x-7}{2}$

$\Rightarrow 2(16x-4-55x+5)=10\times(x-7)$

$\Rightarrow -39x+1=5(x-7)$

$\Rightarrow -39x+1=5x-35$

$\Rightarrow 44x=-36$

$\Rightarrow x=+\frac{36}{44}$

$\Rightarrow x=\frac{9}{11}$

18. (c) I. False II. False III. False IV. False

V. True, $\frac{x}{2}+\frac{x}{5}+\frac{3x}{10}=\frac{1}{5}+\frac{4}{5}$

$\Rightarrow 5x+2x+3x=10$

$\Rightarrow 10x=10$

$\therefore x=1$

Hence, $x=1$ is a solution of given equation.

19. (d)

From option (a), $\frac{3x-5}{6}=\frac{x}{3}\Rightarrow 9x-15=6x$

$\Rightarrow 3x-15\Rightarrow x-5$

From option (b), $\frac{z}{3}-\frac{1}{3}=\frac{4}{3}\Rightarrow\frac{z-1}{3}=\frac{4}{3}\Rightarrow z=5$

From option (c), $6y+7=3y+22$

$\Rightarrow 6y-3y=22-7\Rightarrow 3y=15\Rightarrow y=5$

From option (d), $\frac{7y-1}{4}=\frac{10}{3}$

$\Rightarrow 21y-3=40\Rightarrow 21y=43\Rightarrow y=\frac{43}{21}$

The odd one is option (d), because value of variable is in fraction.

20. (c) From option (a), $\frac{x}{3}-\frac{x}{2}=8\Rightarrow\frac{12}{3}-\frac{12}{2}=8$

[$\because x=12$, given]

$\Rightarrow 4-6=8\Rightarrow -2\neq 8$

From option (b), $\frac{x}{3}-\frac{x}{4}=16\Rightarrow\frac{12}{3}-\frac{12}{4}=16$

[$\because x=12$, given]

$\Rightarrow 4-3=16\Rightarrow 1\neq 16$

From option (c), $\frac{x}{2}+\frac{x}{3}-\frac{x}{4}=7$

$\Rightarrow \frac{12}{2}+\frac{12}{3}-\frac{12}{4}=7$ [$\because x=12$, given]

$\Rightarrow 6+4-3=7\Rightarrow 7=7$

From option (d), $\frac{2x}{3}=\frac{8}{12}-\frac{0.25}{3}$

$\Rightarrow \frac{2\times 12}{3}=\frac{8}{12}-\frac{0.25}{3}$ [$\because x=12$, given]

$\Rightarrow \quad 8 = \frac{2}{3} - \frac{0.25}{3} \Rightarrow 8 = \frac{1.75}{3}$

$\Rightarrow \quad 24 \neq 1.75$

21. (*b*) $3(t-3) = 5(2t+1)$

$\Rightarrow \quad 3t - 9 = 10t + 5$

$\Rightarrow -9 - 5 = 10t - 3t$

$\Rightarrow \quad 7t = -14$

$\Rightarrow \quad t = -\frac{14}{4} = -2$

22. (*d*) From option (d),

$0.25(4f-3) = 0.05(10f-9)$

$\Rightarrow \quad f - 0.75 = 0.05 \times 10f - 0.05 \times 9$

$\Rightarrow \quad f - 0.75 = 0.5f - 0.45$

$\Rightarrow \quad 0.5f = 0.30$

$\Rightarrow \quad f = \frac{0.30}{0.5}$

$\Rightarrow \quad f = 0.6$

Hence, option (d) is satisfied for $f = 0.6$.

23. (*c*) From option (c),

$\frac{2}{x+3} - \frac{4}{x-3} = \frac{-6}{x+3}$

$= \frac{2(x-3) - 4(x+3)}{(x+3)(x-3)} = \frac{-6}{(x+3)}$

$= \frac{2x - 6 - 4x - 12}{(x+3)(x-3)} = \frac{-6}{(x+3)}$

$\Rightarrow \quad \frac{-2x-18}{x-3} = -6$

$\Rightarrow \quad -2x = -6x + 18 + 18$

$\Rightarrow \quad 4x = 36$

$\Rightarrow \quad x = 9$

24. (*b*) I. $2(y+3) + 3(y+1) = 4(2y-3) + 3$

$\Rightarrow \quad 2y + 6 + 3y + 3 = 8y - 12 + 3$

$\Rightarrow \quad 2y + 3y - 8y = -12 + 3 - 6 - 3$

$\Rightarrow \quad -3y = -18$

$\Rightarrow \quad y = 6$

II. Let A be fill in blank.

Then, $5x + \frac{7}{2} = \frac{3}{2}x - A$

Given, $x = -5$

$\Rightarrow \quad 5 \times (-5) + \frac{7}{2} = \frac{3}{2} \times (-5) - A$

$\Rightarrow -25 + \frac{7}{2} + \frac{15}{2} = -A$

$\Rightarrow \quad \frac{-50 + 7 + 15}{2} = -A$

$\Rightarrow \quad A = \frac{28}{2}$

$\Rightarrow \quad A = 14$

III. $\quad \frac{2}{5x} - \frac{5}{3x} = \frac{1}{15}$

$\Rightarrow \quad \frac{6-25}{15x} = \frac{1}{15}$

$\Rightarrow \quad \frac{-19}{15x} = \frac{1}{15}$

$\Rightarrow \quad x = -19$

IV. $\frac{y-1}{3} - \frac{y-2}{4} = 1$

$\Rightarrow \frac{4y - 4 - 3y + 6}{12} = 1$

$\Rightarrow \quad y + 2 = 12$

$\Rightarrow \quad y = 12 - 2 = 10$

25. (*b*) I. $8x - 5 - 3x = 6x - 4x + 4$

$\Rightarrow \quad 5x - 5 = 2x + 4$

$\Rightarrow \quad 5x - 2x = 4 + 5$

$\Rightarrow \quad 3x + 9 \quad \Rightarrow \quad x = 3$

II. Number of solution for a linear equation in one variable is 1.

III. $x = 3 \times 2 = 6$

[The smallest prime number is 2.]

and $x = 11 - 5 = 6$

IV. $\frac{5}{y} + 7 = \frac{2}{y} + 4$

$\Rightarrow \quad \frac{3}{y} = 4 - 7$

$\Rightarrow \quad \frac{3}{y} = -3$

$\Rightarrow \quad y = -1$

Chapter 13 : Geometry

1. (*c*) In ΔBOM,

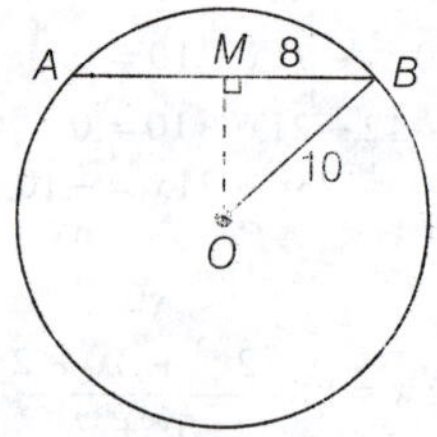

$OB^2 = OM^2 + MB^2$ [By Pythagoras]

$(10)^2 = OM^2 + (8)^2$

$OM^2 = 100 - 64$

$OM = \sqrt{36}$

$OM = 6$ cm

2. (*c*) In ΔLMK and ΔONK

$\angle KML = \angle ONK = 46°$

$\angle K = \angle K$ [common]

$\therefore \Delta LKM \sim \Delta ONK$ [*AA* similarity]

$\Rightarrow \frac{KM}{KN} = \frac{LM}{ON} \Rightarrow \frac{b+c}{c} = \frac{a}{x}$

$\Rightarrow \quad x = \frac{ac}{b+c}$

3. (*a*) Given, $\angle A$ is twice the measure of $\angle B$.

i.e., $\angle A = 2\angle B$

We know, $\angle A + \angle B = 90°$ [complementary angles]

$\Rightarrow \quad 2\angle B + \angle B = 90°$

$\Rightarrow \quad 3\angle B = 90°$

$\Rightarrow \quad \angle B = 30°$

So, $\angle A = 60°$

4. (*a*) Sum of adjacent angles $= 180°$

$\therefore x + 40° + x - 20° = 180°$

$\Rightarrow \quad 2x = 160° \Rightarrow x = 80°$

5. (*b*)

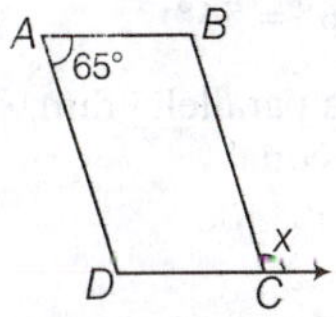

$\because$ Opposite angles of a parallelogram are equal.

$\angle A = \angle C = 65°$

$\therefore \quad \angle x = 180° - 65° = 115°$ [by linear pair]

6. (*a*)

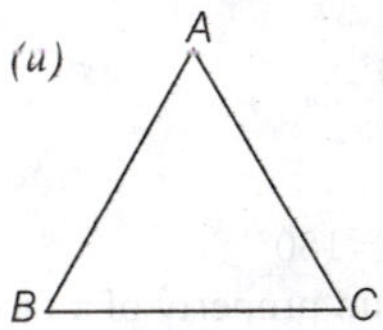

$\therefore$ Given, ΔABC is an isosceles triangle.

Let $\angle B = \angle C = 54°$

$\therefore \quad \angle A + \angle B + \angle C = 180°$ [Angle sum property]

$\Rightarrow \quad \angle A + 54° + 54° = 180°$

$\Rightarrow \quad \angle A = 180° - 108°$

$\Rightarrow \quad \angle A = 72°$

7. (*a*) $\because$ Sum of adjacent angles $= 180°$

$\therefore \quad (2x - 4)° + (3x - 1)° = 180°$

$\Rightarrow \quad 5x = 185°$

$\Rightarrow \quad x = 37°$

$\therefore$ Angles are $(37 \times 2 - 4), (37 \times 3 - 1)$.

$= 37 \times 2 - 4, 37 \times 3 - 1$

$= 70°, 110°$

Since, opposite angles of a parallelogram are equal.

Hence, all angles of a parallelogram are $70°, 110°, 70°, 110°$

8. (*b*) $\because$ Sum of adjacent angles of a parallelogram $= 180°$

$\therefore \quad 7x + 2x = 180°$

$\Rightarrow \quad 9x = 180° \Rightarrow x = 20°$

Hence, angles are $140°, 40°, 140°, 40°$.

9. (*b*) Given, $AC = 10$ cm

$BD = 24$ cm

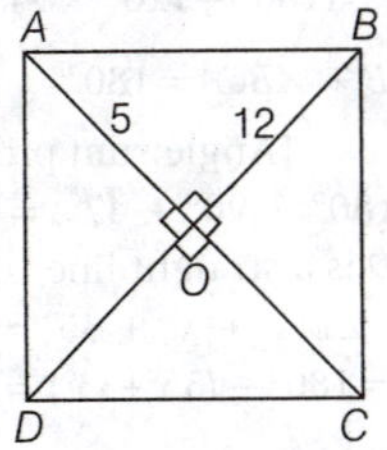

So, $OA = 5$ cm and $OB = 12$ cm

($\therefore$ Diagonals bisect each other)

Use pythagoras theorem in ΔAOB

$OA^2 + OB^2 = AB^2 \Rightarrow 5^2 + 12^2 = AB^2$

$AB = \sqrt{25 + 144}$

$AB = \sqrt{169} \Rightarrow AB = 13$ cm

10. (*d*) We have diagonal of a rectangle are equal and bisect each other.

$\therefore$ In ΔAOB, $\angle AOB = 162 - 3x$ [verticle opposite angles]

$\angle OBA = \angle OAB = 2x \quad (\because OA = OB)$

$\therefore \angle AOB + \angle OBA + \angle OAB = 180°$

$\Rightarrow \quad 162° - 3x + 2x + 2x = 180°$

$\Rightarrow \quad x = 18°$

11. (*c*) $\therefore$ Opposite angles of a rhombus are equal

$2x + 15° = 3x - 30° \Rightarrow x = 45°$

Now,

In ΔBCD, $CD = CB$

$\Rightarrow \quad \angle CBD = \angle BDC$

Also, $\angle DCB = 3 \times 45° - 30° = 105°$

$\therefore \quad \angle BDC = \frac{180° - 105°}{2} = \frac{75°}{2} = 37.5°$

12. (*c*) In ΔAOQ and ΔBOP, we have

$\angle OAQ = \angle OBP$ [Each equal to 90°]

$\angle AOQ = \angle POB$ [Vertically opposite angles]

$\therefore$ By AA- similarity,

$\Delta AOQ \sim \Delta BOP$

$\Rightarrow \quad \frac{AO}{BO} = \frac{OQ}{OP} = \frac{AQ}{BP}$

$\Rightarrow \quad \frac{AO}{BO} = \frac{AQ}{BP} \Rightarrow \frac{10}{6} = \frac{AQ}{9}$

$\Rightarrow \quad AQ = \frac{10 \times 9}{6} = 15$ cm

13. (*b*) Given $\angle OBA = 36°$

$\Rightarrow \angle ODC = 36°$ [$\because AB \parallel CD$, DB is the transversal, alternate angles are equal]

and $\angle COD = 90°$ [$\because$ Diagonals of a rhombus bisect each other at right angles]

$\therefore$ In ΔCOD, $x = \angle OCD = 180 - (\angle ODC + \angle COD)$

$\Rightarrow \quad x = 180 - (36° + 90°)$

$= 180° - 126° = 54°$

14. (*b*) $\angle A + \angle B + \angle BCA = 180°$

[Angle sum property of triangle]

$\Rightarrow \angle BCA = 180° - (90° + 47°) = 43°$

Since, $\angle ACD$ is a straight line

$\Rightarrow \quad \angle BCA + x° + 35° = 180°$

$\Rightarrow \quad x = 180° - (35° + 33°) = 102°$

15. (*b*)

I. **Rectangle** Opposite sides are equal and all angles are 90°.

II. **Square** : All sides are equal and all angles are 90°.

III. **Rhombus** All sides are equal.

IV. **Trapezium** : One pair of opposite sides are parallel.

16. (*a*) I. False

II. True, the sum of all exterior angles of a polygon is 360°.

III. True

IV. True, because, sum of interiar angles of a polygon = $(2n - 4) \times 90°$

or $\quad (n-2) \times 180°$

17. (*b*) Using property, sum of all exterior angles of a polygon is 360°.

$\therefore \quad x + y + z + w = 360°$

18. (*b*) Since, opposite angles of a parallelogram are equal.

$\therefore \quad \angle S = \angle Q, \angle P = \angle R$

$\angle Q = 180° - 60° = 120°$

[$\because \angle PQR + \angle RQY = 180°$]

$\therefore \quad \angle S = \angle Q = 120°$

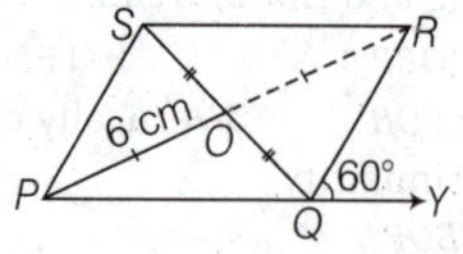

$\because$ Sum of all angles of parallelogram $PQRS$ = 360°

$\therefore \angle P + \angle R = 360° - 2 \times 120° = 120°$

$2\angle P = 120°$

$\Rightarrow \angle P = 60° = \angle R \quad \therefore \angle S : \angle R = 120° : 60° = 2 : 1$

19. (*a*) According to the property of rectangle,

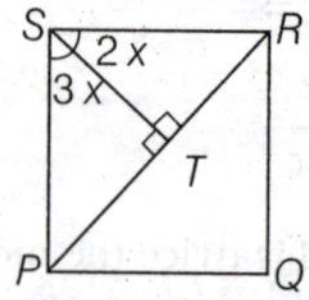

$3x + 2x = 90°$

$\Rightarrow \quad 5x = 90°$

$\Rightarrow \quad x = 18°$

$\therefore \quad 3x = 3 \times 18° = 54°$

and $\quad 2x = 2 \times 18° = 36°$

In ΔPTS,

$54° + 90° + \angle TPS = 180°$

[$\because$ sum of angles of triangle is 180°]

$\Rightarrow \angle TPS = 180° - 144° = 36°$

$\therefore \quad \angle TPQ = 90° - 36° = 54°$

20. (*d*) Given, $ABCD$ is a parallelogram, so their opposite angles are equal

$\therefore \quad \angle ADC = \angle ABC$

$\Rightarrow \quad x = z$

Now, in right angled traingle EBC, we have

$\angle BEC + \angle EBC + \angle ECB = 180°$

[use angle sum property of a triangle]

$\Rightarrow \; 90° + x + 40° = 180°$

$\Rightarrow \; x = 180° - 130° = 50°$

From Eq, (i), $x = z = 50°$

Now, in ΔFCD, we have

$\angle CFD + \angle FDC + \angle FCD = 180°$

[use angle sum property of a triangle]

$\Rightarrow \quad 90° + 50° + \angle FCD = 180°$

$\Rightarrow \; \angle FCD = 180° - 140° = 40°$

Also, in parallelogram $ABCD$, sum of adjust angles is 180°.

$\therefore \quad \angle ADC + \angle DCB = 180°$

$\Rightarrow 50° + (\angle FCD + y + 40°) = 180°$

$\Rightarrow \quad 50° + 40° + y + 40° = 180°$

$\Rightarrow \quad y = 180° - 130° \Rightarrow y = 50°$

$\therefore \quad x = y = z = 50°$

21. (*a*)

I. Sum of the interior angles of Quadrilateral is 360°.

II. Square is a regular quadrilateral.

III. In an equilateral triangle, each angle is 60°.

IV. In a rhombus diagonals intersect at 90°.

V. Length of other diagonal is 6 cm. because diagonals of rectangle are equal.

Chapter 14 : Area and Perimeter

1. (c) The area of the remaining sheet after the smaller circle is removed will be = Area of the entire circle with radius 14 cm – Area of the circle with radius 5 cm.
We know, Area of circle = πr^2
So, Area of the entire circle = $\pi(14)^2 = 196\pi\ cm^2$
And, Area of the circle with radius 5 cm which is cut out = $\pi(5)^2 = 25\pi\ cm^2$
Thus, the remaining area $= 196\pi - 25\pi$
$= 171\pi\ cm^2$

2. (b) When the wire is bent into a square.
Side $= 132 \div 4 = 33$ cm
Area of the square = $(\text{side})^2 = (33)^2 = 1089\ cm^2$
When the wire is bent into a circle.
Circumference = $2\pi r$
$\Rightarrow \quad 132 = 2\pi r$
$\Rightarrow \quad 132 = 2 \times \frac{22}{7} \times r \Rightarrow 132 \times \frac{7}{44} = r$
$\Rightarrow \quad r = 21$ cm
We know, area of circle = πr^2
$= \frac{22}{7} \times 21 \times 21 = 1386\ cm^2$
So, the circle will have a larger area.

3. (d) Let the side of the square be x cm.
Area = $(\text{side})^2 = x^2\ cm^2$
If its side becomes $3x$ cm then area = $(3x)^2$
$= 9x^2\ cm^2$
Ratio is $x^2 : 9x^2 = 1 : 9$
Hence, the area would become nine times.

4. (d) Given : $d_1 = 24$ cm, $d_2 = 10$ cm
$\therefore$ Side of the rhombus $= \frac{1}{2}\sqrt{d_1^2 + d_2^2}$
$= \frac{1}{2} \times \sqrt{(24)^2 + (10)^2}$
$= \frac{1}{2} \times \sqrt{576 + 100} = \frac{1}{2} \times \sqrt{676}$
$= \frac{1}{2} \times 26 = 13$ cm
The perimeter of square = $4 \times$ side
$= 4 \times 13 = 52$ cm
Hence, the perimeter = 52 cm.

5. (b) Length of the rectangle = 23 cm
Breadth of the rectangle = 12 cm
When they are doubled,
$l = 23 \times 2 = 46$ cm
and $b = 12 \times 2 = 24$ cm
Perimeter $= 2(l + b) = 2(46 + 24) = 2 \times 70$
$= 140$ cm

6. (a) Perimeter (P) of square
$= 4 \times$ Side of the square
Hence, P (square) $= 4 \times 35 = 140$ cm
Perimeter of rectangle
$= 2 \times$ (Length + Breadth)
Hence, P (rectangle) $= 2 \times (25 +$ Breadth)
$= 50 + 2 \times$ Breadth
According to the given question,
$50 + 2 \times$ Breadth $= 140$ cm
$\Rightarrow \quad 2 \times$ Breadth $= 140 - 50$
$\Rightarrow \quad$ Breadth $= \frac{90}{2}$
The breadth of the rectangle = 45 cm
Now, the area of rectangle = Length $\times$ Breadth
$= 45 \times 25 = 1125\ cm^2$

7. (c) Let the breadth of the wall = h m
$\therefore$ Height of the wall = $5h$ m
Length of the wall = $40h$ m
$\therefore 40h \times 5h \times h = 18225$
$\Rightarrow \quad 200 \times h^3 = 18225$
$\Rightarrow \quad h^3 = 91.125$
$\Rightarrow \quad h = 4.5$ m

8. (c) The dimensions of the cuboid are in the ratio 1 : 2 : 3.
Let the dimensions be x, $2x$, $3x$ in metres.
Total surface area = $132\ m^2$
$\Rightarrow \quad 132 = 2(lb + bh + hl)$
$\Rightarrow \quad 132 = 2(x \times 2x + 2x \times 3x + 3x \times x)$
$\Rightarrow \quad 132 = 2(2x^2 + 6x^2 + 3x^2)$
$\Rightarrow \quad 66 = 11x^2$
$\Rightarrow \quad x^2 = 6 \Rightarrow \quad x = 6$ m
$\therefore$ So, dimensions of cuboid are $x = 6$ m,
$2x = 2 \times 6 = 12$ m
and $3x = 3 \times 6 = 18$ m

9. (a) Let the sides of the three cubes be $3K$, $4K$, and $5K$ respectively.
$\therefore$ Volume of the new cube formed by melting the three cubes
$= (3K)^3 + (4K)^3 + (5K)^3$
$= 27K^3 + 64K^3 + 125K^3 = 216K^3$
$\Rightarrow$ Each edge of the new cube
$= \sqrt[3]{216K^3} = 6K$
$\therefore$ Diagonal of the new cube $= 6K\sqrt{3}$

Given, $6K\sqrt{3} = 12\sqrt{3}$

$\Rightarrow \quad 6K = 12 \Rightarrow K = 2$

$\therefore$ Sides of the three cubes are 6 cm, 8 cm and 10 cm respectively.

10. (a) Total surface area of the cube
$= 6a^2 = 6 \times 1^2 = 6$ sq. units

$DB = \sqrt{AD^2 + AB^2} = \sqrt{1+1} = \sqrt{2}$

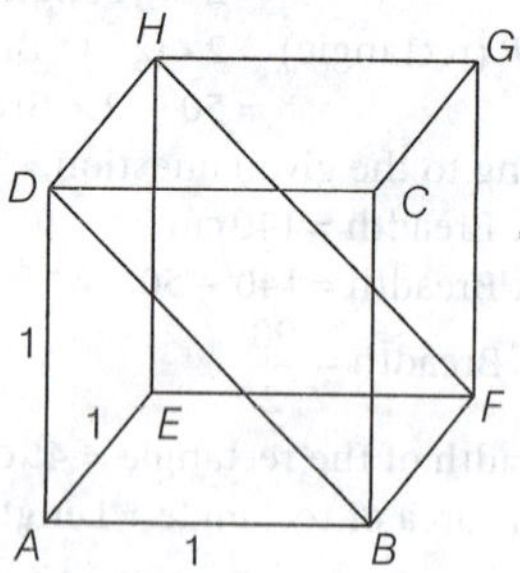

Surface area of the section $DBFH$
$= DB \times BF = \sqrt{2} \times 1$ sq. units
$= \sqrt{2}$ sq. units

$\therefore$ Total surface area of one part $= \frac{6}{2} + \sqrt{2}$
$= (3 + \sqrt{2})$ sq units

11. (b) Let $ABCD$ be the rhombus as shown below.

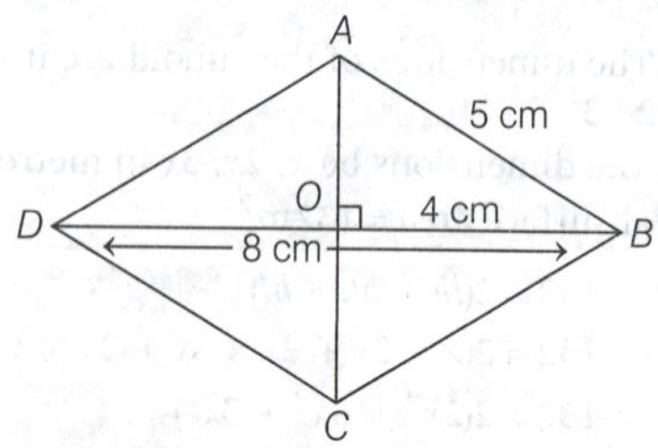

$DO = OB = 4$ cm, since diagonals of a rhombus are perpendicular bisectors of each other.
Therefore, using pythagoras theorem in ΔAOB,

$AO^2 + OB^2 = AB^2$

$AO = \sqrt[2]{AB^2 - OB^2}; \quad AO = \sqrt[2]{5^2 - 4^2}$

$AO = \sqrt[2]{25 - 16}; \quad AO = \sqrt[2]{9}$

$AO = 3$ cm; $\quad AC = AO \times 2 = 3 \times 2 = 6$ cm

Area of rhombus $= \frac{1}{2} \times d_1 \times d_2$

$= \frac{1}{2} \times 8 \times 6 = 24 \text{ cm}^2$

where, $d_1 = AC$; $d_2 = BD$, diagonals of a rhombus

12. (d) Let the length, breadth and height of the cuboid be l, b and h respectively.

$l \times b = 60,\ b \times h = 72,\ l \times h = 120$

$\therefore l \times b \times b \times h \times l \times h = 60 \times 72 \times 120$

$\Rightarrow \quad l^2b^2h^2 = 60 \times 36 \times 2 \times 60 \times 2$

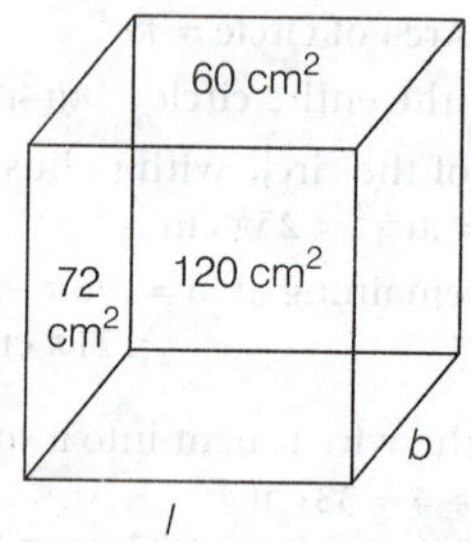

$\therefore$ Volume of the cuboid $= lbh$
$= \sqrt{l^2b^2h^2} = \sqrt{60 \times 36 \times 2 \times 60 \times 2}$
$= 60 \times 6 \times 2 \text{ cm}^3 = 720 \text{ cm}^3$

13. (a) Let 'h' be the height of the wall.

Area of four walls $= 2(l + b)\,h \text{ m}^2$
$= 2(20 + 16)\,h \text{ m}^2 = 72h \text{ m}^2$

Sum of the areas of the floor and the flat roof
$= 20 \times 16 + 20 \times 16 = 640 \text{ m}^2$

Given, that the sum of the areas of four walls is equal to the sum of the areas of the floor and roof

$72h = 640$

$h = \frac{640}{72} = \frac{80}{9}$ m

Volume of the hall $= 20 \times 16 \times \frac{80}{9} \text{ m}^3$
$= 2844.44 \text{ m}^3$

14. (d) Given, Length of the box $l = 4$ m,
Breadth of box, $b = 3$ m
Height of box, $h = 2$ m
We know that, the surface area of a cuboid
$= 2(lb + bh + lh)$

But here the bottom part is not to be painted.
So, Surface area of box to be pained
$= lb + 2(bh + hl)$
$= 4 \times 3 + 2(3 \times 2 + 2 \times 4)$
$= 12 + 2(6 + 8)$
$= 12 + 28 = 40 \text{ m}^2$

Hence, the required surface area of the cuboidal box $= 40 \text{ m}^2$

15. (a)

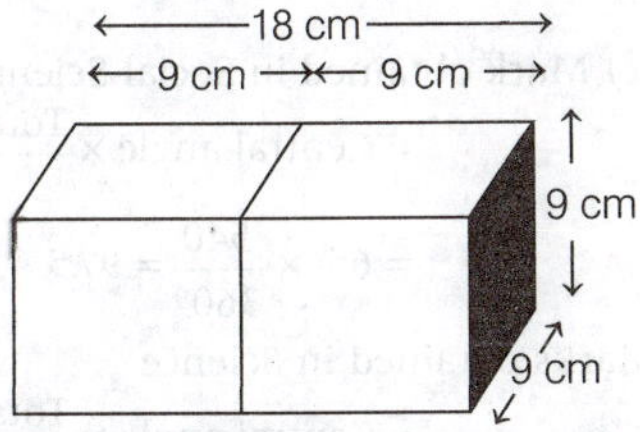

Length of each cube = 9 cm

Length of the resulting cuboid = 9 + 9 = 18 cm

Breadth = 9 cm

Height = 9 cm

Volume of the cuboid = $l \times b \times h$

$= 18 \times 9 \times 9 = 1458\ \text{cm}^3$

16. (c) $h = 1.25\,\text{m}, r = \frac{35}{100}\,\text{m} = 0.35\,\text{m}$

The area of metal used = Total surface area of the box $= 2\pi r(h + r)$

$= 2 \times \frac{22}{7} \times 0.35(1.25 + 0.35)\ \text{m}^2$

$= \left(2 \times \frac{22}{7} \times 0.35 \times 1.6\right)\text{m}^2$

$= 3.52\,\text{m}^2$

The cost of material used = ₹ (3.52 × 80)

= ₹ 281.60

17. (a) Volume of water $= 160\ \text{m}^3$

Area of rectangular field $= 800\ \text{m}^2$

Let h be the height of water level in the field.

Now, the volume of water = volume of cuboid formed on the field by water.

160 = Area of base × height = 800 × h

$\Rightarrow \quad h = 0.2\,\text{m} = 20\ \text{cm}$

So, required height = 20 cm

18. (c) Converting into same units, we have

Length of the wall = 36 m = 36 × 100 = 3600 cm

Breadth of the wall = 4 m = 4 × 100 = 400 cm and thickness of wall = 30 cm

length of the brick = 24 cm

breadth = 15 cm and height = 12 cm

Number of bricks required $= \frac{\text{Volume of wall}}{\text{Volume of one brick}}$

$= \frac{3600 \times 400 \times 30}{24 \times 15 \times 12} = 10000$

Hence, the required number of bricks = 10000

19. (b) Volume of the cube 1 with side 6 cm

$= (\text{side})^3 = (6)^3 = 216\ \text{cm}^3$

Volume of the cube 2 with side 8 cm

$= (\text{side})^3 = (8)^3 = 512\,\text{cm}^3$

Volume of the cube 3 with side 10 cm

$= (\text{side})^3 = (10)^3 = 1000\ \text{cm}^3$

Volume of big cube = volume of cube 1 + volume of cube 2 + volume of cube 3

Volume of the big cube $= 216\,\text{cm}^3 + 512\,\text{cm}^3 + 1000\ \text{cm}^3 = 1728\ \text{cm}^3$

Side of the resulting cube $= \sqrt[3]{1728} = 12\,\text{cm}$

Total surface area $= 6\ (\text{side})^2 = 6(12)^2$

$= 6 \times 144\ \text{cm}^2 = 864\ \text{cm}^2$

20. (b) Breadth of rectangular sheet becomes circumference of base (circular part) of cylinder

Circumference of the base $= 2\pi r$

$22 = \frac{2 \times 22 \times r}{7} \Rightarrow r = \frac{7}{2}$

Volume of cylinder $= \pi r^2 h$

Now, length of rectangular sheet becomes height of cylinder

$= \frac{22}{7} \times \frac{7}{2} \times \frac{7}{2} \times 50 = 1925\,\text{cm}^3$

Hence, the required volume $= 1925\,\text{cm}^3$.

21. (c) The volume of the earth dug out $= \pi r^2 h$

$= \left(\frac{22}{7} \times 3.5 \times 3.5 \times 16\right)\text{m}^3 = 616\ \text{m}^3$

[∴ Earth comes out in the shape of cylinder]

The area of the given plot $= (22 \times 7)\ \text{m}^2$

$= 154\ \text{m}^2$

The volume of the platform formed = The volume of the earth dug out $= 616\ \text{m}^3$

The height of the platform $= \frac{\text{volume}}{\text{area}}$

$= \frac{616}{154} = 4\ \text{m}$

The height of the platform = 4 m

22. (a)

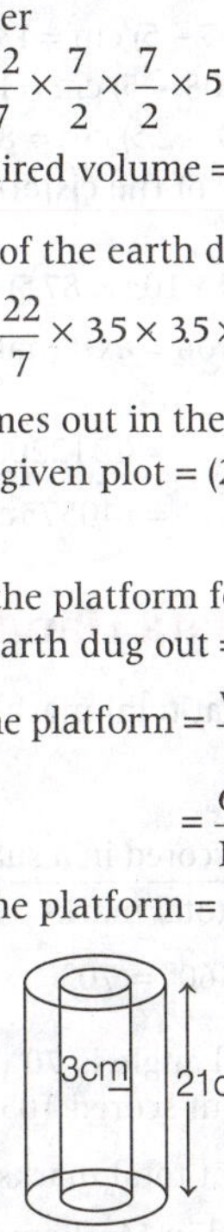

The external radius of the pipe, $R = 4$ cm

The internal radius of the pipe, $r = (4 - 1)$ cm

$= 3\,\text{cm}$

The external volume $= \pi R^2 h$

$= \left(\frac{22}{7} \times 4 \times 4 \times 21\right)\text{cm}^3$

$= 1056\ \text{cm}^3$

The internal volume $= \pi r^2 h$

$$= \left(\frac{22}{7} \times 3 \times 3 \times 21\right) \text{cm}^3$$

$$= 594 \text{ cm}^3$$

The volume of the metal = external volume − internal volume

$$= (1056 - 594) \text{ cm}^3$$

$$= 462 \text{ cm}^3$$

The weight of the pipe $= (462 \times 8)$ g

$$= \frac{462 \times 8}{1000} \text{ kg} = 3.696 \text{ kg}$$

23. *(c)* The external dimensions of the cistern are length = 135 cm, breadth = 108 cm, depth = 90 cm.

External volume $= (135 \times 108 \times 90) \text{ cm}^3$

$$= 1312200 \text{ cm}^3$$

The internal dimensions of the cistern are

Length = (135 − 5) cm = 130 cm,

Breadth = (108 − 5) cm = 103 cm

Height = (90 − 2.5) cm = 87.5 cm

The capacity of the cistern = internal volume of the cistern

$$= (130 \times 103 \times 87.5) \text{ cm}^3 = 1171625 \text{ cm}^3$$

Volume of iron = external volume − internal volume

$$= (1312200 - 1171625) \text{ cm}^3$$

$$= 140575 \text{ cm}^3$$

Chapter 15 : Data Handling

1. *(b)* Given that total marks scored by students = 540

Central angle

$$= \frac{\text{Marks scored in a subject}}{\text{total marks}} \times 360°$$

$$= \frac{105}{540} \times 360° = 70°$$

Since central angle is 70°, thus we found that in Hindi, student scored 105 marks.

2. *(c)* Given that total marks = 540

Marks scored in Mathematics

$$= \text{Central angle} \times \frac{\text{Total marks}}{360}$$

$$= 90° \times \frac{540}{360°} = 135$$

And marks scored in Hindi = 105

Thus marks obtained by the student in Mathematics more than Hindi = 135 − 105 = 30

3. *(c)* Mark obtained in Social Science

$$= \text{Central angle} \times \frac{\text{Total Marks}}{360}$$

$$= 65° \times \frac{540}{360°} = 97.5$$

Marks obtained in Science

$$= \text{Central angle} \times \frac{\text{Total Marks}}{360°}$$

$$= 80° \times \frac{540}{360°} = 120$$

So, marks obtained in Social Science and Mathematics

$$= 97.5 + 135 = 232.5 \quad \ldots\text{(i)}$$

and marks obtained in Science and Hindi

$$= 120 + 105 = 225 \quad \ldots\text{(ii)}$$

Thus marks obtained by the student in sum of Social Science and Mathematics more than sum of marks of Science and Hindi.

$$= 232.5 - 225 = 7.5 \text{ marks}$$

4. *(a)* The seven boys who failed the test scored the marks less than those given marks. Let the marks be $x_1, x_2, x_3, x_4, x_5, x_6, x_7$.

Then, the marks arranged in ascending order are $x_1, x_2, x_3, x_4, x_5, x_6, x_7$, 12, 15, 15, 15, 16, 17, 17, 18, 18, 19, 19, 19

$$\therefore \text{ Median score} = \left(\frac{19+1}{2}\right)\text{th item}$$

$$= 10\text{th item} = 15$$

5. *(d)* Sector angle corresponding to recreation

$$= 360° - (72° + 90° + 54°)$$

$$= 360° - 216°$$

$$= 144°$$

∴ Percentage expenses incurred on account of

$$\text{recreation} = \left(\frac{144°}{360} \times 100\right)\% = 40\%$$

6. *(b)* Let the number of boys be x and the number of girls be y.

$$\text{Then, } \frac{70 \times x + 55 \times y}{(x + y)} = 60$$

$$\Rightarrow \quad 70x + 55y = 60x + 60y$$

$$\Rightarrow \quad 10x = 5y$$

$$\Rightarrow \quad \frac{x}{y} = \frac{5}{10} = \frac{1}{2}$$

$$\Rightarrow \quad x : y = 1 : 2$$

7. *(b)* ∴ The most common mode of Transport is bus.

8. *(a)* By Car $= \frac{90°}{360°} = \frac{1}{4}$; By Cycle $= \frac{60°}{360°} = \frac{1}{6}$

9. (d) Let total Children be x. Then,

$$\frac{18}{x} = \frac{90°}{360°}$$

$$\Rightarrow \quad x = 72$$

10. (b) Percentage of Indian students

$$= \frac{180°}{360°} \times 100 = 50\%$$

11. (a) Percentage of African students

$$= \frac{45°}{360°} \times 100 = 12\frac{1}{2}\%$$

12. (d) Central angle for others students is 45°.

So fraction is $\frac{45°}{360°} = \frac{1}{8}$.

13. (a) $\frac{120°}{540°} = \frac{x}{360°} \Rightarrow x = 80°$

In English the student score 120 marks.

14. (a) Difference between marks obtained in Math and English

$$= \frac{(90° - 80°)}{360°} \times 540$$

$$= \frac{10°}{360°} \times 540 = 15 \text{ marks}$$

15. (d) The angle is minimum for Hindi. So, thats why Hindi is the subject in which the student got minimum marks.

16. (a) ∴ Number of cars emit pollutin below 45.5 is

$$= 4 + 10 + 14 = 28$$

17. (c) ∴ Number of cars emit pollution more than 55.5 = 14 + 2 = 16

18. (d) ∴ The range of pollution emit by 10 cars = 35.5-40.5.

19. (c) Day 1, Day 3, Day 5 and Day 8 i.e. 4 days have actual high temperatures with respect to its prediction.

20. (d) Day 2 and Day 6 i.e. 2 days have actual temperatures and it prediction is same.

21. (a) Days 8,
Predicted temperature : 30°
⇒ Actual temperature : 36°
Deviation → 36° – 30° = 6°
which is maximum.

22. (b) Total number of elementary events = 6
Favourable number of elementary events = 2 (i.e. 3, 6)

∴ Required probability

$$= \frac{\text{Favourable number of elementary events}}{\text{Total number of elementary events}}$$

$$= \frac{2}{6} = \frac{1}{3}$$

23. (a) Total number of elementary events = 52
Number of favourable elementary events = 2
[spade ace and Diamondace]

∴ Required probability $= \frac{2}{52} = \frac{1}{26}$

24. (c) Expenditure incurred on cement

$$= \frac{\text{Central angle} \times \text{total cost}}{360°}$$

$$\Rightarrow \text{Total cost of flat} = \frac{360° \times 112500}{75°}$$

$$= ₹\ 540000$$

25. (a) ∴ Expenditure incurred on labour

$$= \frac{\text{Central angle} \times \text{total cost}}{360°}$$

$$= \frac{100° \times 540000}{360°} = ₹\ 150000$$

26. (c) We have,
Expenditure incurred on cement = ₹ 112500
and total cost of flat = 540000

$$\Rightarrow \text{Required ratio} = \frac{112500}{540000} = \frac{1125}{5400} = \frac{5}{24}$$

⇒ 5 : 24

27. (c) $\frac{100}{600} = \frac{x}{360°}$

$$x = 60°$$

28. (a) $\frac{50 + 150}{600} = \frac{x}{360°}$

$$\Rightarrow \frac{200}{600} = \frac{x}{360°}$$

$$x = 120° \text{ or fraction} = \frac{1}{3}$$

29. (b) ∴ Activity chosen by highest number of student is swimming and central angle

$$\frac{300}{600} = \frac{x}{360°} \Rightarrow x = 180°$$

30. (d) Total number of marbles in a jar
= 8 + 6 + 7 + 6 = 27
Number of red marbles = 6
∴ Probability of choosing a red marble

$$= \frac{6}{27} = \frac{2}{9}$$

Practice Set 1

1. (b) Given, $\frac{a}{b} = \frac{4}{5} \Rightarrow a = \frac{4b}{5}$ ... (i)

and $a + b = 27$ ... (ii)

From Eqs. (i) and (ii), we get

$$\frac{4}{5}b + b = 27$$

$$\Rightarrow \frac{9}{5}b = 27 \Rightarrow b = 15$$

$$\therefore a = \frac{4 \times 15}{5} = 12$$

So, $a \times b = 15 \times 12 = 180$

2. (d) Consider, $\frac{\sqrt{441} + \sqrt{196}}{\sqrt{1024} - \sqrt{324}} = \frac{21 + 14}{32 - 18} = \frac{35}{14} = \frac{5}{2}$

3. (c) Let $\frac{a}{b}$ be the rational number.

$\therefore$ Its multiplicative inverse $= \frac{b}{a}$

So, we have $\frac{a}{b} \times \frac{b}{a} = 1$

4. (b) Given, *RENT* is a rectangle with diagonals *RN* and *ET*.

Since diagonals of a rectangle are equal and bisect each other.

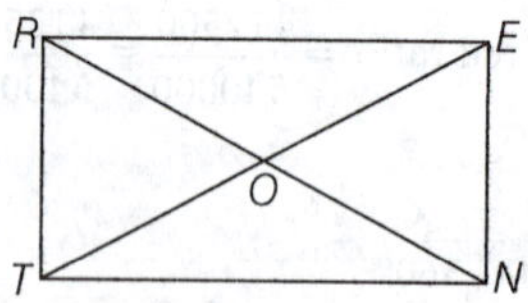

$\therefore \quad 2x + 4 = 3x + 1 \Rightarrow x = 3$

5. (a) Let printed price be ₹ 100.

Then, SP after 10% discount = ₹ (100 − 10) = ₹ 90

Profit per cent earned 12%

CP of article $= \frac{100 \times \text{SP}}{(100 + \text{Profit\%})}$

$= ₹ \frac{100}{112} \times 90 = ₹ \frac{1125}{14}$

$\therefore$ Ratio of CP : Printed price $= \frac{1125}{14} : 100 = 45 : 56$

6. (d) There are only five cubes of 3-digit i.e. 125, 216, 343, 512, 729.

Only sum of digits of 216 is a perfect square.

i.e. $2 + 1 + 6 = 9 = 3^2$

7. (c) $3^m \div 3^{-3} = 3^4$

$\Rightarrow \quad 3^m = 3^4 \times 3^{-3} \Rightarrow 3^m = 3^1$

$\Rightarrow \quad m = 1$ [by comparing]

8. (b) Given $x * y = x + y - \sqrt{xy}$

$\therefore \quad 7 * 63 = 7 + 63 - \sqrt{7 \times 63} = 70 - 21 = 49$

9. (b) Given, $x^2 - (a + b)x + ab$

$a^2 + b^2 = 20$ [given

and $a^2 - b^2 = 12$ [given]

On solving above equations, we get

$a = 4, b = 2$ [where, $a, b > 0$]

$\therefore$ Expression $= x^2 - 6x + 8$

10. (c) In case of compound interest, we know

$$A = P\left(1 + \frac{r}{100}\right)^t$$

$$1331 = 1000\left(1 + \frac{10}{100}\right)^t$$

$$\frac{1331}{1000} = \left(\frac{110}{100}\right)^t \Rightarrow \left(\frac{11}{10}\right)^3 = \left(\frac{11}{10}\right)^t$$

$$\Rightarrow \quad t = 3\,\text{yr}$$

11. (d) Given, area of Square $= (\text{Side})^2 = 19600$

Side = 140 m

Diagonal = Side $\times \sqrt{2} = 140\sqrt{2}$ m

12. (c) Let the three numbers be a, b and c.

According to the question,

$$a + b + c = 105$$

$$\frac{a}{b} = \frac{2}{3} \text{ and } \frac{b}{c} = \frac{4}{5}$$

We have,

$$b = \frac{4}{5}c$$

Also, $\frac{a}{b} \times \frac{b}{c} = \frac{2}{3} \times \frac{4}{5} \Rightarrow \frac{a}{c} = \frac{8}{15}$

$$\therefore \quad a = \frac{8}{15}c$$

So, we have $\frac{8}{15}c + \frac{4}{5}c + c = 105$

$\Rightarrow \quad 8c + 12c + 15c = 105 \times 15$

$\Rightarrow \quad 35c = 105 \times 15$

$\Rightarrow \quad c = 3 \times 15 = 45$

So, $b = \frac{4}{5} \times 45 = 36$

13. (d) Consider,

$$[(24^2 + 7^2)^{1/2}]^3 = [(625)^{1/2}]^3$$
$$= [25]^3 = 15625$$

14. (a) Consider, $y^3 - 2y^2 - 9y + 18$

$$= y^2(y - 2) - 9(y - 2) = (y^2 - 9)(y - 2)$$

Divide both RHS and LHS by $(y - 2)$

So, $\frac{y^3 - 2y^2 - 9y + 18}{y - 2} = \frac{(y^2 - 9)(y - 2)}{y - 2}$

$[\because a^2 - b^2 = (a + b)(a - b)]$

$= y^2 - 9 = (y - 3)(y + 3)$

15. (*b*) Let angles be $3x$ and $2x$.

Then, $3x + 2x = 180° \Rightarrow x = 36°$

$\therefore$ Angle opposite to $\angle A = 3x = 3 \times 36° = 108°$

16. (*c*) Given, $z - \frac{z - 2 + 2z}{4} = 2z - \frac{4 + 3z}{2}$

$(4z - z + 2 - 2z)\,2 = (4z - 4 - 3z)\,4$

$\Rightarrow (4z - z + 2 - 2z) = 2(4z - 4 - 3z)$

$\Rightarrow z + 2 = 2(z - 4)$

$\Rightarrow z + 2 = 2z - 8 \Rightarrow 10 = z$

17. (*c*) Only zero is the number which has nonreciprocal because $\frac{1}{0}$ is not defined.

18. (*c*) Consider, $\sqrt{41 - \sqrt{29 - \sqrt{18 - \sqrt{4}}}}$

$= \sqrt{41 - \sqrt{29 - \sqrt{18 - 2}}}$

$= \sqrt{41 - \sqrt{29 - \sqrt{16}}} = \sqrt{41 - \sqrt{29 - 4}}$

$= \sqrt{41 - \sqrt{25}} = \sqrt{41 - 5} = \sqrt{36} = 6$

19. (*a*) Given $\frac{7.25 \times 7.25 \times 7.25 + 1.75 \times 1.75 \times 1.75}{9}$

$= \frac{(7.25)^3 + (1.75)^3}{9}$

Using identity, $(a^3 + b^3) = (a + b)(a^2 + b^2 - ab)$

$= \frac{(7.25 + 1.75)[(7.25)^2 + (1.75)^2 - (7.25)(1.75)]}{9}$

$= \frac{9(5256 + 3.06 - 1269)}{9} = 42.93$

20. (*b*) Both Statements I and II are needed to answer the question.

21. (*d*) $(2^{3x-1} + 10) \div 6 = 7$

$\Rightarrow 2^{3x-1} + 10 = 7 \times 6$

$\Rightarrow 2^{3x-1} = 42 - 10$

$\Rightarrow 2^{3x-1} = 2^5 \quad [\because 32 = 2^5]$

$\Rightarrow 3x - 1 = 5 \quad$ [by comparing]

$\Rightarrow 3x = 6$

$\Rightarrow x = 2$

22. (*b*) Given, $7 + 3x = 7 - 3x$

$6x = 0$

$x = 0$

So, $7x^2 + 4x + 9 = 7 \times 0 + 4 \times 0 + 9 = 9$

23. (*c*) The expression given in the question, Follows the property distribution of multiplication over addition.

24. (*c*) $\frac{25 \times a^{-4}}{5^{-3} \times 10 \times a^{-8}} = x \times a^4$

$\Rightarrow \frac{(5)^2}{5^{-3} \times 5 \times 2} \times a^4 = x \times a^4$

$\Rightarrow \frac{5^{2+3-1}}{2} \times a^4 = x \times a^4$

$\Rightarrow \frac{1}{2} \times 5^4 \times a^4 = x \times a^4$

$\Rightarrow x = \frac{1}{2} \times 5^4$

25. (*c*) $(3^{-4} + 4^{-3} + 5^{-1} + 6^{-2} + 7^{-1})^0 = 1 \quad [\therefore (x)^0 = 1]$

26. (*b*) $\sqrt[3]{\sqrt{0.015625}} = (0.015625)^{1/6}$

$= \left(\frac{15625}{1000000}\right)^{1/6} = \left[\left(\frac{5}{10}\right)^6\right]^{1/6}$

$= \left(\frac{5}{10}\right)^{6 \times \frac{1}{6}} = \frac{5}{10} = 0.5$

27. (*b*) Given, $P = ₹700$, $A = ₹\,952$, $t = 3$ yr.

$SI = A - P = 952 - 700 = 252$

$SI = \frac{P \times r \times t}{100}$

$252 = \frac{700 \times r \times 3}{100}$

$36 = 3r$

$r = 12\%$

Given, rate increased by 25%.

$\therefore$ 125% of $12 = \frac{125}{100} \times 12 = 15\%$

Now, new rate = 15%,

$P = 800$, $t = 3$ yr

$\therefore SI = \frac{800 \times 3 \times 15}{100} = 360$

$A = P + SI = 800 + 360 = ₹1160$

28. (*b*) Given, $xyz = 8$

$x + y + z = 8$

$\therefore \frac{1}{xy} + \frac{1}{yz} + \frac{1}{xz} = \frac{x + y + z}{xyz} = \frac{8}{8} = 1$

29. (*b*) Let the two numbers be x and y.

Given,

$5 \times x = 6 \times y$

$\frac{x}{y} = \frac{6}{5}, \; x : y = 6 : 5$

Let numbers are 6m and 5m.
Then, according to the question, $x + y = 11$

$$6\text{m} + 5\text{m} = 11$$
$$11\text{m} = 11$$
$$m = 1$$

$\therefore$ Bigger number = 6 m, i.e., = $6 \times 1 = 6$

30. *(c)* Let the number of rows = x

Given,
Number of rows = Number of flowers in each row.
Total flowers = Number of rows × number of flowers in a row.

$$x \times x = 9604$$
$$x^2 = 9604$$

Taking square root of both sides,

$$x = \sqrt{9604} = 98$$

31. *(b)* $V = \pi(R^2 - r^2)h = \frac{22}{7}(8^2 - 5^2)\left(3\frac{1}{2}\right)$

$$= \frac{22}{7}(64 - 25)\left(\frac{7}{2}\right)$$
$$= 11 \times 39 = 429$$

32. *(b)* Given,

$$6 : 8 : : x : 15$$
$$\text{i.e.,} \ \frac{6}{8} = \frac{x}{15}$$
$$x = \frac{15 \times 6}{8} = \frac{45}{4}$$

33. *(d)* Shape given in question consisting a cone surmounted on a cylinder.

34. *(a)* Division of two rational number is closed under rational numbers.

35. *(d)* Given, $R = 6\%$, SI = 300

$$\text{SI} = \frac{P \times r \times t}{100}$$
$$\Rightarrow \quad 300 = \frac{P \times 6 \times 2}{100}$$
$$P = ₹2500$$

Now, $A = P\left(1 + \frac{r}{100}\right)^t$

$$A = 2500\left(1 + \frac{6}{100}\right)^2 = 2500 \times \frac{106}{100} \times \frac{106}{100}$$
$$A = ₹2809$$
$$\text{CI} = \text{A} - \text{P} = ₹2809 - ₹2500$$
$$= ₹309$$

36. *(c)* Given, weight and length of rod is directly propotional.
If $l = 6$ m, $w = 30$ kg
If $l = 7$ m, $w = 35$kg
So, on increasing length 1 m, the weight of rod is increases 5 kg.
So, length of 1 m rod = $\frac{30}{6} = 5$kg.
Similarly, length of 25m long rod = 25×5
$= 125$kg

37. *(b)* Length of the diagonals is equal in square and bisect each other at right angles.

38. *(d)* (iii) $(x + y) \times (x^2 - xy + y^2)$

$$= x^3 - x^2y + xy^2 + x^2y - xy^2 + y^3$$
$$= x^3 + y^3$$

(iv) $2x(z - x - y)$

$$= 2xz - 2x^2 - 2xy$$

Hence, (iii) and (iv) are incorrect multiplication.

39. *(c)* Factors of 33075 = $5 \times 5 \times 3 \times 3 \times 3 \times 7 \times 7$

$\therefore$ For making cube, 3 same digits is compulsory in each number.
So, $5 \times 7 = 35$ is the least number should be multiplied to obtain a perfect cube.

40. *(b)* Given, $\frac{17 - 3x}{5} - \frac{4x + 2}{3} = 5 - 6x + \frac{7x + 14}{3}$

Multiplying by LCM of 5 and 3 on both sides.
$\therefore$ LCM of 5 and 3 = 15

$$\Rightarrow 3(17 - 3x) - 5(4x + 2) = 15(5 - 6x) + 5(7x + 14)$$
$$\Rightarrow 51 - 9x - 20x - 10 = 75 - 90x + 35x + 70$$
$$\Rightarrow 41 - 29x = 145 - 55x$$
$$\Rightarrow -29x + 55x = 145 - 41$$
$$\Rightarrow 26x = 104$$
$$\Rightarrow x = \frac{104}{26}$$
$$\Rightarrow x = 4$$

41. *(b)* Given expression is

$$\left(\frac{3}{5}x^2y\right) \times \left(\frac{-15}{4}xy^2\right) \times \left(\frac{7}{9}x^2y^2\right)$$
$$= \left[\frac{3}{5} \times \left(-\frac{15}{4}\right) \times \frac{7}{9}\right](x^2 \times x \times x^2) \times (y \times y^2 \times y^2)$$
$$= \frac{-7}{4}x^5y^5 \quad \text{...(i)}$$

On putting $x = 2$ and $y = -1$ in Eq. (i), we get

$$\frac{-7}{4}(2^5)(-1)^5 = \frac{7}{4} \times 32 = 56$$

42. (*b*) Given,

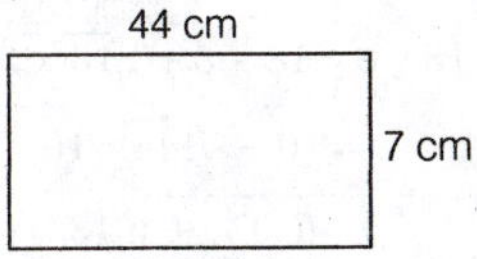

If we fold rectangular sheet then length become the circumference of circular part of cylinder.

$$2\pi r = 44$$

$$\Rightarrow \quad 2\times\frac{22}{7}\times r = 44$$

$$r = 7\text{ cm}, h = 7\text{ cm}$$

Volume of cylinder $= \pi r^2 h = \frac{22}{7}\times 7\times 7\times 7$

$= 22\times 49 = 1078\text{ cm}^3$

43. (*b*) Given, $\angle DPC = 110^\circ$ and $\angle BCD = 80^\circ$

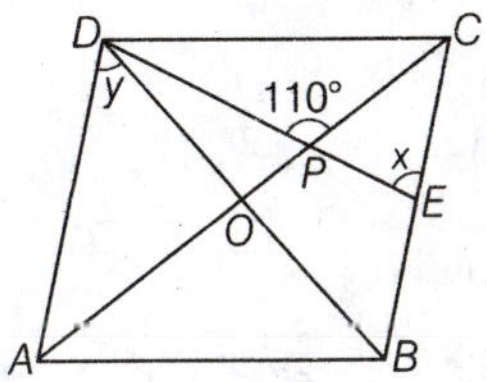

In ΔDOP,

$\angle DOP + \angle ODP = 110^\circ$

[exterior angle theorem]

$\therefore 90^\circ + \angle ODP = 110^\circ$

[diagonals of rhombus intersect each other at 90°]

$\therefore \quad \angle ODP = 20^\circ$

Now, $AD || BC$ and DE is the transversal.

$\because \quad \angle x = \angle y + 20^\circ$

From the given options, only option (b) satisfies the relation.

44. (*c*) Given, $\frac{1}{5} : \frac{1}{x} = \frac{1}{x} : \frac{1}{125}$

Then, $\dfrac{\frac{1}{5}}{\frac{1}{x}} = \dfrac{\frac{1}{x}}{\frac{1}{125}}$

$\Rightarrow \quad \frac{x}{5} = \frac{125}{x}$

$\Rightarrow \quad x^2 = 125\times 5$

$\Rightarrow \quad x = 25$

45. (*c*) Total number of elementary events = 40

Number of favourable elements = 10

[i.e. 4, 8, 12, 16, 20, 24, 28, 32, 36, 40]

$\therefore$ Required probability $= \frac{10}{40} = \frac{1}{4}$

46. (*c*) Given 4% of P = 12% of Q

$\Rightarrow \quad \frac{4}{100}\times P = \frac{12}{100}\times Q$

$\Rightarrow \quad 4P = 12Q \quad \Rightarrow \quad \frac{P}{Q} = \frac{12}{4} = \frac{3}{1}$

$\Rightarrow \quad P : Q = 3 : 1$

Again given, 8% of Q = 16% of R

$\Rightarrow \quad \frac{8}{100}\times Q = \frac{16}{100}\times R \Rightarrow 8Q = 16R$

$\Rightarrow \quad \frac{Q}{R} = \frac{16}{8} = \frac{2}{1}$

$\Rightarrow \quad Q : R = 2 : 1$

Now, $\quad P : Q = 3 : 1$ and $Q : R = 2 : 1$

$\Rightarrow \quad P : Q = 3\times 2 : 1\times 2$ and $Q : R = 2 : 1$

$\Rightarrow \quad P : Q = 6 : 2$ and $Q : R = 2 : 1$

Then, $P : Q : R = 6 : 2 : 1$

Again given R's income = ₹ 2000

Let the total income = ₹x

Then, $\quad \frac{1}{6+2+1}\times x = 2000$

$x = 2000\times 9$

$x -$ ₹18000

47. (*b*) Given,

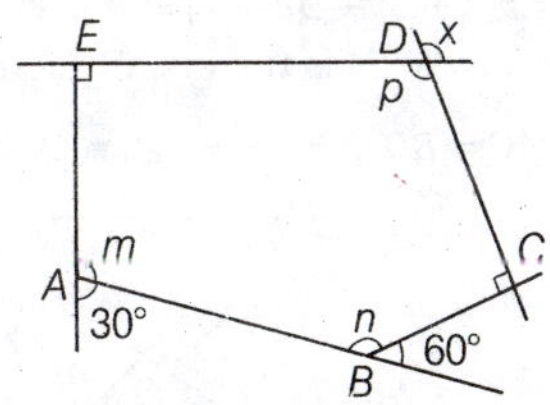

We know, $\angle m + 30^\circ = 180^\circ$

(Angle in a straight line)

$\angle m = 150^\circ$

$\angle n + 60^\circ = 180^\circ$ (Angle in a straight line)

$\angle n = 120^\circ$

We know, if sides = 5 = n, then sum of interior angles is $[(n-2)\times 180^\circ] = (5-2)\times 180^\circ = 540^\circ$

$\therefore \quad 90^\circ + \angle m + \angle n + 90^\circ + \angle p = 540$

$[\angle p = x$ (vertically opposite angle)$]$

$\Rightarrow \quad 90^\circ + 150^\circ + 120^\circ + 90^\circ + \angle x = 540^\circ$

$\angle x = 540 - 450^\circ$

$\angle x = 90^\circ$

48. (*d*) Let the age of man is $10y + x$.

and age of his wife will be $10x + y$.

According to the question,

Sum of man and his wife age = 99

$10y + x + 10x + y = 99$

$\Rightarrow \quad 11x + 11y = 99$

$\Rightarrow \quad x + y = \frac{99}{11} = 9$

$\therefore \quad x + y = 9 \quad \ldots \text{(i)}$

Now, According to question again,

$$(10y + x) = (10x + y) + 9$$
$$9y - 9x = 9$$
$$y - x = 1 \quad \ldots \text{(ii)}$$

On solving Eqs. (i) and (ii), we get

$$y = 5, x = 4$$

$\therefore$ Men's age $= 10y + x$

$$= 10 \times 5 + 4 = 54$$

49. (*d*) 10% represents 20 people.

$\Rightarrow$ 100% represents $= \left(\dfrac{100}{10} \times 20\right) = 200$

Therefore, 200 people were surveyed.

50. (*c*) CD's of semi-classical music

$$= \left(\frac{20}{100} \times 1000\right) = 200$$

2. Practice Set

1. (*c*) $p^2 + 6p - 16$

$$= p^2 + 8p - 2p - 16$$
$$= p(p + 8) - 2(p + 8) = (p + 8)(p - 2)$$

Hence, $(p - 2)$ is the one of factor of $p^2 + 6p - 16$.

2. (*b*) $AC = BD + 5$ [given]

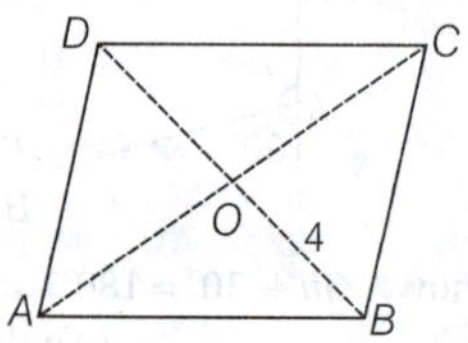

$\because$ Diagonals of a parallelogram bisect each other.

$\therefore \quad OA = OC$ and $OB = OD$

$\therefore \quad BD = 4 + 4 = 8$

Also, $\quad AC = OA + OC$

$$= 8 + 5 = 13$$

$\therefore \quad OA = \dfrac{AC}{2} = \dfrac{13}{2} = 6.5$

3. (*a*) $\dfrac{7y + 4}{y + 2} = -\dfrac{4}{3}$

$\Rightarrow 3(7y + 4) = -4(y + 2)$

$\Rightarrow 21y + 12 = -4y - 8$

$\Rightarrow 21y + 4y = -8 - 12$

$\Rightarrow \quad 25y = -20$

$\Rightarrow \quad y = -\dfrac{20}{25}$

$$y = -\frac{4}{5}$$

4. (*b*) Given, $p * q = p - q + \sqrt{pq}$

$\therefore \quad 18 * 8 = 18 - 8 + \sqrt{18 \times 8}$

$$= 10 + \sqrt{144} = 10 + 12 = 22$$

5. (*b*) We have, $\sqrt{\dfrac{(0.02)^2 + (0.18)^2 + (0.42)^2}{(0.002)^2 + (0.018)^2 + (0.042)^2}}$

$$= \sqrt{\frac{\left(\frac{2}{100}\right)^2 + \left(\frac{18}{100}\right)^2 + \left(\frac{42}{100}\right)^2}{\left(\frac{2}{1000}\right)^2 + \left(\frac{18}{1000}\right)^2 + \left(\frac{42}{1000}\right)^2}}$$

$$= \sqrt{\frac{[(2)^2 + (18)^2 + (42)^2]}{[(2)^2 + (18)^2 + (42)^2]} \times \frac{(1000)^2}{(100)^2}}$$

$$= \frac{1000}{100} = 10$$

6. (*c*) Given expression is

$$\frac{2}{5} \times \left(-\frac{8}{9}\right) + p \times \frac{5}{9} = \frac{2}{5} \times [q + r]$$

From option (c),

On putting $p = -\dfrac{2}{5}, q = -\dfrac{8}{9}, r = -\dfrac{5}{9}$

Then, $\dfrac{2}{5} \times \left(-\dfrac{8}{9}\right) + \left(\dfrac{-2}{5}\right) \times \dfrac{5}{9} = \dfrac{2}{5} \times \left[\dfrac{-8}{9} + \dfrac{(-5)}{9}\right]$

$\Rightarrow \dfrac{2}{5} \times \left(\dfrac{-8}{9}\right) + \dfrac{(-10)}{45} = \dfrac{2}{5} \times \dfrac{(-8)}{9} + \dfrac{2}{5} \times \dfrac{(-5)}{9}$

$\Rightarrow \quad \dfrac{-16}{45} - \dfrac{10}{45} = \dfrac{-16}{45} - \dfrac{10}{45}$

LHS = RHS

7. (*b*) Total number of elementary events = 52

Number of favourable events = 2

$\therefore$ Required Probability $= \dfrac{2}{52} = \dfrac{1}{26}$

8. (*d*) Let CP of article be x.

According to the question,

$$317 - x = x - 233$$

$\Rightarrow \quad 2x = 550$

$\Rightarrow \quad x =$ ₹ 275

CP of article = ₹ 275

Profit per cent = 20% [given]

$\therefore$ New SP $= 275 \times \dfrac{120}{100} =$ ₹ 330

9. (*c*) According to the question,

$$\frac{\text{Sum of exterior angle}}{\text{Sum of interior angle}} = \frac{1}{5}$$

$\Rightarrow \quad \dfrac{360^\circ}{(n - 2) \times 180^\circ} = \dfrac{1}{5}$

$\Rightarrow \quad (n-2)\times 180° = 360\times 5$

$n-2 = 5\times 2$

$\Rightarrow \quad n-2 = 10 \Rightarrow n = 12$

10. (*d*) We have, $\sqrt{\dfrac{(0.0144)\times(0.0289)}{(0.0025)\times(0.0441)}}$

$$= \sqrt{\frac{(0.12)^2\times(0.17)^2}{(0.05)^2\times(0.21)^2}} = \frac{0.12\times 0.17}{0.05\times 0.21}$$

$$= \frac{12\times 17}{5\times 21} = \frac{4\times 17}{5\times 7} = \frac{68}{35}$$

11. (*b*) In step III, $n = 3$ and rate of interest should be $r = \dfrac{10}{2} = 5\%$

$\because$ Interest compounded half-yearly.

$\therefore$ Steps III and IV both are wrong.

12. (*a*) Given, $\dfrac{a}{b} = \dfrac{4}{3}$

Consider $\dfrac{a^2+b^2}{a^2-b^2} = \dfrac{\left(\dfrac{a}{b}\right)^2+1}{\left(\dfrac{a}{b}\right)^2-1} = \dfrac{\left(\dfrac{4}{3}\right)^2+1}{\left(\dfrac{4}{3}\right)^2-1}$

$$= \frac{\frac{16+9}{9}}{\frac{16-9}{9}} = \frac{25}{7}$$

13. (*b*) $\left(\dfrac{5}{3}\right)^{-4}\times\left(\dfrac{5}{3}\right)^{-5} = \left(\dfrac{5}{3}\right)^{3y}\times\left(\dfrac{5}{3}\right)^{0}$

$$\left(\frac{5}{3}\right)^{-4-5} = \left(\frac{5}{3}\right)^{3y}\times 1 \Rightarrow \left(\frac{5}{3}\right)^{-9} = \left(\frac{5}{3}\right)^{3y}$$

Comparing exponent both sides, we get

$-9 = 3y \Rightarrow y = -3$

14. (*c*) Let the number of notes be x.

According to the question,

$2x\times 100 + 3x\times 500 + 5x\times 1000 = 20100$

$\Rightarrow \quad 200x + 1500x + 5000x = 20100$

$\Rightarrow \quad 6700x = 20100$

$\Rightarrow \quad x = 3$

Hence, number of ₹ 500 denomination

$= 3\times 3 = 9$

15. (*c*) We have, $\dfrac{2}{5}\times\dfrac{5}{2} - \dfrac{2}{5}\times\dfrac{5}{4} = 1 - \dfrac{1}{2} = \dfrac{1}{2}$

16. (*b*) $28\sqrt{x} + 1426 = \dfrac{3}{4}\times 2872$

$28\sqrt{x} + 1426 = 2154$

$28\sqrt{x} = 728 \Rightarrow \sqrt{x} = 26$

$x = 676$ (Squaring on both sides)

17. (*a*) Let the digit at ten's place be x.

Original number $= 10x + (11 - x)$

So, new number $= (11 - x)\times 10 + x$

According to the question,

$(110 - 10x + x) - (10x + 11 - x) = 27$

$\Rightarrow \quad 110 - 9x - 9x - 11 = 27$

$\Rightarrow \quad 99 - 18x = 27$

$\Rightarrow \quad 99 - 27 = 18x$

$\Rightarrow \quad 72 = 18x$

$\therefore \quad x = 4$

Hence, new number $= (11 - 4)\times 10 + 4$

$= 70 + 4 = 74$

18. (*b*) Let three consecutive integers be x, $(x + 1)$ and $(x + 2)$ when taken in decreasing order and multiplied by 5, 6 and 7, respectively.

According to the question,

$5(x+2) + 6(x+1) + 7x = 214$

$\Rightarrow \quad 5x + 10 + 6x + 6 + 7x = 214$

$\Rightarrow \quad 18x + 16 = 214$

$\Rightarrow \quad 18x = 198$

$\Rightarrow \quad x = \dfrac{198}{18}$

$\Rightarrow \quad x = 11$

$\therefore$ Numbers are 11, 12 and 13.

So, average of the numbers $= \dfrac{11+12+13}{3}$

$= \dfrac{36}{3} = 12$

19. (*c*) The given expression is

$15pq + 15 + 9q + 25p$

$= 15pq + 25p + 15 + 9q$

$= 5p(3q + 5) + 3(5 + 3q)$

$= (3q + 5)(5p + 3)$

$= 1\cdot(3q + 5)(5p + 3)$

Here, 1, $(3q + 5)$ and $(5p + 3)$ are three factor of given expression.

Hence, $(3p + 5)$ is not factor of given expression.

20. (*c*) CP of 11 books = ₹ 10

SP of 10 books = ₹ 11

CP of 110 books = ₹ 10 × 10 = ₹ 100

SP of 110 books = ₹ 11 × 11 = ₹ 121

Profit = ₹ (121 − 100) = ₹ 21

$\therefore$ Profit per cent $= \dfrac{21}{100}\times 100 = 21\%$

21. (*b*) Let the number be x.

According to the question,

$$\left(\frac{2}{3}\right)x\times\frac{3}{4} = 6$$

$\Rightarrow \quad \frac{6}{12}x = 6 \Rightarrow x = \frac{6 \times 12}{6}$

$\therefore \quad x = 12$

22. (*a*) For compounded half yearly, $r = \frac{r}{2}$

$t = 2t$

Money paid by Manish $= 2000\left(1 + \frac{10}{100}\right)^2$

$= 2000\left(\frac{11}{10}\right)\left(\frac{11}{10}\right) = 121 \times 20 = ₹\,2420$

$\therefore$ For compounded $\frac{1}{4}$th year, $r = \frac{r}{4}$, $t = 4t$

Money received by Manish $= 2000\left(1 + \frac{5}{100}\right)^4$

$= 2000\left(\frac{21}{20}\right)^4$

$= 2000 \times \frac{21 \times 21 \times 21 \times 21}{20 \times 20 \times 20 \times 20}$

$= ₹\,2431.01$

$\therefore$ Amount gained by Manish

$= ₹\,2431.01 - ₹\,2420 = ₹\,11.01$

23. (*b*) Consider

$x - \frac{x+1}{4} = 2 - \frac{x-3}{3}$

$\Rightarrow \quad \frac{4x - x - 1}{4} = \frac{6 - x + 3}{3}$

$\Rightarrow \quad \frac{3x - 1}{4} = \frac{9 - x}{3}$

$\Rightarrow \quad 9x - 3 = 36 - 4x$

$\Rightarrow \quad 13x = 39$

$\therefore \quad x = \frac{39}{13} = 3$

24. (*b*) Ratio $= \frac{\frac{1}{3} \text{ of } ₹9.30}{0.6 \text{ of } ₹1.55}$

$= \frac{\frac{1}{3} \times ₹9.3}{0.6 \times ₹1.55} = \frac{31}{0.6 \times 1.55}$

$= \frac{3.1}{0.93} = \frac{10}{3}$

25. (*c*) Simplified value of $\frac{250}{625} = \frac{2}{5}$

$\therefore$ Additive inverse of $\frac{2}{5} = -\frac{2}{5}$

26. (*c*) Nearby to get perfect square of 2200 we consider as 2209. So, 9 should be added to make it a perfect square.

27. (*d*) All the steps involved in the factorisation of a polynomial given in the question is correct. Hence, option (d) is correct.

28. (*a*)

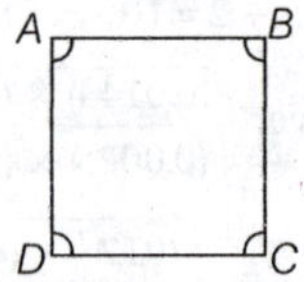

Three angles are equal. i.e.

$\angle A = \angle B = \angle C = x$ (let)

Also given $\quad \angle D = 120°$

Since, $\angle A + \angle B + \angle C + \angle D = 360°$

(Angle sum property of a quadrilateral)

$\Rightarrow x + x + x + 120° = 360°$

$\Rightarrow \quad 3x = 240°$

$\Rightarrow \quad x = 80°$

29. (*d*) $\left(\frac{4}{25} \times \frac{2}{5}\right) - \frac{64}{25} = \frac{8}{125} - \frac{64}{25} = \frac{8 - 320}{125} = -\frac{312}{125}$

Hence, option (d) is correct.

30. (*a*) Let the number be x.

Reciprocal of that number $= \frac{1}{x}$

According to the given condition, $x - \frac{1}{x} = 5$

Cubing both sides, we get

$\left(x - \frac{1}{x}\right)^3 = (5)^3$

$\Rightarrow x^3 - \frac{1}{x^3} - 3x \times \frac{1}{x}\left(x - \frac{1}{x}\right) = 125$

$\Rightarrow \quad x^3 - \frac{1}{x^3} = 125 + 3 \times 5 = 140$

31. (*b*) Ratio of age of 3 persons $= 1 : 2 : 3$

$\therefore$ Let age of youngest $= 1x$

Let age of middle $= 2x$

Let age of eldest $= 3x$

$\therefore$ Sum of youngest and eldest $= 60$ yr.

$\therefore \quad 1x + 3x = 60$

$4x = 60$

$x = 15$

Age of eldest $= 3x = 3 \times 15 = 45$ yr

32. (*c*) Let the sum of money be x

Amount $= 3 \times ₹x = ₹3x$

Interest = Amount – Principal

$= ₹3x - ₹x = ₹2x$

Rate $= 13\frac{1}{3}\%$ p.a. $= 40/3\%$ p.a.

$\text{SI} = \frac{P \times R \times T}{100}$

$$\text{Time }(T) = \left(\frac{\text{SI} \times 100}{(P \times R)}\right)$$
$$= \frac{(2x \times 100)}{x \times (40/3)} \text{ yr} = \frac{(2 \times 100 \times 3)}{40} \text{ yr}$$
$$= \frac{(100 \times 3)}{20} \text{ yr} = 15 \text{ yr}$$

33. (*b*) Given, $5^{2x+1} \div 25 = 125$

$$\Rightarrow \frac{5^{2x+1}}{(5)^2} = 125 \Rightarrow 5^{2x+1-2} = (5)^3$$

Here, base is same, so exponent will be same.

$\therefore$ $2x + 1 - 2 = 3$

$\Rightarrow$ $2x = 4$

$\Rightarrow$ $x = 2$

34. (*c*) Let the angles of triangles are $= 1x, 2x, 3x$

$\therefore$ Sum of all angles of triangle $= 180°$

[Angle sum property of triangle]

$\therefore$ $(1x + 2x + 3x) = 180°$

$\Rightarrow$ $6x = 180°$

$\Rightarrow$ $x = 30°$

$\therefore$ Sum of smallest and greatest angles

$= x + 3x = 4x$

$= 4° \times 30° = 120°$

35. (*d*) $\because$ Additive Inverse of $-\frac{5}{2} = \frac{5}{2}$

$\therefore$ Reciprocal of $(-1) = -\frac{1}{1} = (-1)$

product $= \frac{5}{2} \times (-1) = -\frac{5}{2}$

$\therefore$ Multiplicative Inverse of product $= -\frac{2}{5}$

36. (*a*) Article sold by Ragini at 20% profit for ₹180

$x \times \frac{120}{100} = 180$ [x = CP Ist]

$\Rightarrow$ $x = ₹150$

Article sold at 25% loss, then

$y \times \frac{75}{100} = 150$ [y = CP 2nd]

$\Rightarrow$ $y = ₹200$

Overall CP = 150 + 200 = 350

Overall SP = 180 + 150 = 330

Loss = CP − SP = ₹350 − ₹330 = ₹20

Loss per cent $= \frac{20}{350} \times 100 = 5.71\%$

37. (*a*) Given, $A : B = 3 : 4$, $B : C = 8 : 9$,

$C : D = 15 : 16$

Now, $A : B = 3 \times 2 : 4 \times 2$, $B : C = 8 : 9$

$\therefore$ $A : B : C = 6 : 8 : 9$

$= 6 \times 5 : 8 \times 5 : 9 \times 5$,

Also, $C : D = 15 : 16 = 15 \times 3 : 16 \times 3$

$A : B : C : D = 30 : 40 : 45 : 48$

$\therefore$ $A : D = 30 : 48$

$\Rightarrow$ $A : D = 5 : 8$

38. (*c*) Let the number be x.

According to the question,

$$x \times \frac{4}{5} + \frac{2x}{3} = -\frac{11}{5}$$

$$\Rightarrow \frac{12x + 10x}{15} = -\frac{11}{5}$$

$$\Rightarrow \frac{22x}{3} = -11$$

$$\therefore x = -\frac{3}{2}$$

39. (*d*) Given expression is

$$\left(\frac{3}{4}a^2 + 3b^2\right) \times 4\left(a^2 - \frac{2}{3}b^2\right)$$

$$= \frac{3}{4}a^2\left(4a^2 - \frac{8}{3}b^2\right) + 3b^2\left(4a^2 - \frac{8}{3}b^2\right)$$

$$= \frac{3}{4}a^2 \times 4a^2 - \frac{3}{4}a^2 \times \frac{8}{3}b^2 + 3b^2 \times 4a^2 - 3b^2 \times \frac{8}{3}b^2$$

$$= 3a^4 - 2a^2b^2 + 12a^2b^2 - 8b^4$$

$$= 3a^4 + 10a^2b^2 - 8b^4$$

40. (*d*) Consider, $20z\sqrt{z^3 - 2z^2}$

$= 20z \times z\sqrt{z - 2} = 20 \times 36 \times \sqrt{6 - 2}$

[put $z = 6$]

$= 20 \times 36 \times 2 = 1440$

41. (*a*) Consider,

$$\frac{-\sqrt{\left(\frac{5}{3}\right)^2 \times \left(\frac{3}{5}\right)^2}}{-\sqrt{\left(\frac{2}{5}\right)^3 \times \left(\frac{2}{5}\right)^{-3}}} = \frac{-\sqrt{\left(\frac{5}{3}\right)^{2-2}}}{-\sqrt{\left(\frac{2}{5}\right)^{3-3}}}$$

$$= \frac{-1}{-1} = 1$$

42. (*a*) In parallelogram $RISK$, $\angle K = 120°$

$\therefore$ $\angle R = 180° - 120° = 60°$

[$\because$ Sum of adjacent angles of a parallelogram is 180°]

$\angle S = \angle R = 60°$

[$\because$ opposite angles of a parallelogram are equal]

And in parallelogram $CLUE$,

$\angle L = \angle E = 70°$

In ΔOES, $\angle E + \angle S + \angle O = 180°$

$\Rightarrow \quad 70° + 60° + \angle O = 180°$

$\Rightarrow \quad 130° + x = 180°$

$\therefore \quad x = 50°$

43. *(b)* $\therefore \sqrt{15625} = 125$

Now, $\sqrt{156.25} + \sqrt{1.5625}$

$= \sqrt{\frac{15625}{100}} + \sqrt{\frac{15625}{10000}}$

$= \frac{\sqrt{15625}}{\sqrt{100}} + \frac{\sqrt{15625}}{\sqrt{10000}}$

$= \frac{125}{10} + \frac{125}{100} = 12.5 + 1.25$

$= 13.75$

44. *(b)* $\left(\sqrt{\frac{225}{729}} - \sqrt{\frac{25}{144}}\right) \div \sqrt{\frac{16}{81}}$

$= \left(\sqrt{\frac{15 \times 15}{27 \times 27}} - \sqrt{\frac{5 \times 5}{12 \times 12}}\right) \div \sqrt{\frac{4 \times 4}{9 \times 9}}$

$= \left(\frac{15}{27} - \frac{5}{12}\right) \div \frac{4}{9}$

$= \left(\frac{15}{27} - \frac{5}{12}\right) \times \frac{9}{4}$

$= \frac{15}{27} \times \frac{9}{4} - \frac{5}{12} \times \frac{9}{4}$

$= \frac{15}{12} - \frac{15}{16} = \frac{60 - 45}{48} = \frac{15}{48}$

45. *(a)* Given,

$(a + b) : (b + c) : (c + a) = 6 : 7 : 8$ [Let x]

Now, sum of given ratio

$a + b + b + c + c + a = 6x + 7x + 8x$

$2(a + b + c) = 21x$

Also given, $a + b + c = 14$

$\therefore \quad 2 \times 14 = 21x$

$x = \frac{4}{3}$

$\therefore \quad a + b = 6x = 6 \times \frac{4}{3} = 8$

$\because \quad a + b + c = 14$

$\therefore \quad c = 14 - 8$

$c = 6$

46. *(d)* Given,

$\frac{3t - 2}{4} - \frac{2t + 3}{3} = \frac{2}{3} - t$

$= \frac{3(3t - 2) - 4(2t + 3)}{12} = \frac{2}{3} - t$

$\Rightarrow \quad \frac{9t - 6 - 8t - 12}{12} = \frac{2}{3} - t$

$\Rightarrow \quad \frac{t - 18}{12} = \frac{2 - 3t}{3}$

$\Rightarrow \quad t - 18 = 4(2 - 3t)$

$\Rightarrow \quad t - 18 = 4 \times 2 - 12t$

$\Rightarrow \quad 13t = 26 \Rightarrow t = 2$

Hence, option (d) is incorrect.

47. *(c)* Given perimeter of figure = 57 cm

Perimeter of figure = $2p + 7p + 3p + 2p + 5p$

$19p = 57$

$p = 3$

$\therefore$ Perimeter of triangle = $7p + 3p + 5p = 15p$

$= 15 \times 3 = 45$ cm

48. *(b)* 32 students watched TV for 4-5 h.

Therefore, the maximum number of students watched TV for 4-5 h.

49. *(a)* The number of students who watched TV less than 4 h

$= 22 + 8 + 4 = 34$

50. *(d)* The number of students who spent more than 5 h watching TV = $8 + 6 = 14$.